ECONOMIC GROWTH AND MACROECONOMIC DYNAMICS

Interest in growth theory was rekindled in the mid-1980s with the development of the endogenous growth model. In contrast to the earlier neoclassical model in which the steady-state growth rate was tied to population growth, long-run endogenous growth emerged as an equilibrium outcome, reflecting the behavior of optimizing agents in the economy. This book brings together a number of contributions in growth theory and macroeconomic dynamics that reflect these more recent developments and the ongoing debate over the relative merits of neoclassical and endogenous growth models. It focuses on three important aspects that have been receiving increasing attention. First, it develops a number of growth models that extend the underlying theory in different directions. Second, it addresses one of the concerns of the recent literature on growth and dynamics, namely the statistical properties of the underlying data and the effort to ensure that the growth models are consistent with the empirical evidence. Third, macrodynamics and growth theory have focused increasingly on international aspects, an inevitable consequence of the increasing integration of the world economy.

Steve Dowrick is Professor and Australian Research Council Senior Fellow in the School of Economics, Australian National University. He is coeditor with Ian McAllister and Riaz Hassan of *The Cambridge Handbook of Social Sciences in Australia* (Cambridge University Press, 2003) and author of numerous papers in leading journals in economics including the *American Economic Review*, the *Review of Economics and Statistics*, and the *Economic Journal*. A Fellow of the Australian Academy of Social Sciences, Professor Dowrick's current research focuses on the factors promoting as well as deterring convergence for economic growth.

Rohan Pitchford teaches economics in the Asia Pacific School of Economics and Management of the Australian National University. His research interests are in law and economics, industrial organization, and contract theory and application, including creditor liability and the economics of combining assets. Dr. Pitchford's papers have appeared in the *American Economic Review*, the *Journal of Economic Theory*, and the *Journal of Law, Economics, and Organization*, among other refereed publications.

Stephen J. Turnovsky is Castor Professor of Economics at the University of Washington, Seattle, and previously taught at the Universities of Pennsylvania, Toronto, and Illinois, Urbana-Champaign, and the Australian National University. Elected a Fellow of the Econometric Society in 1981, he coedited with Mathias Dewatripont and Lars Peter Hansen the Society's three-volume *Advances in Economics and Econometrics: Theory and Applications, Eighth World Congress* (Cambridge University Press, 2003). He has written four books, including *International Macroeconomic Dynamics* (MIT Press, 1997) and *Methods of Macroeconomic Dynamics: Second Edition* (MIT Press, 2000), and many journal articles. His current research in macroeconomic dynamics and growth covers both closed and open economies.

Economic Growth and Macroeconomic Dynamics

Recent Developments in Economic Theory

Edited by

STEVE DOWRICK
Australian National University

ROHAN PITCHFORD
Australian National University

STEPHEN J. TURNOVSKY
University of Washington

CAMBRIDGE
UNIVERSITY PRESS

PUBLISHED BY THE PRESS SYNDICATE OF THE UNIVERSITY OF CAMBRIDGE
The Pitt Building, Trumpington Street, Cambridge, United Kingdom

CAMBRIDGE UNIVERSITY PRESS
The Edinburgh Building, Cambridge CB2 2RU, UK
40 West 20th Street, New York, NY 10011-4211, USA
477 Williamstown Road, Port Melbourne, VIC 3207, Australia
Ruiz de Alarcón 13, 28014 Madrid, Spain
Dock House, The Waterfront, Cape Town 8001, South Africa

http://www.cambridge.org

First published 2004

Printed in the United States of America

Typeface Times Ten 10/13 pt.   *System* LATEX 2_ε [TB]

A catalog record for this book is available from the British Library.

Library of Congress Cataloging in Publication Data
Economic growth and macroeconomic dynamics: recent developments in economic
theory / edited by Steve Dowrick, Rohan Pitchford, Stephen J. Turnovsky.
p.   cm.
ISBN 0-521-83561-5 (hardbound)
1. Economic development.   2. Macroeconomics.   3. Statics and dynamics
(Social sciences)   4. Economics.   I. Dowrick, Steve.
II. Pitchford, Rohan.   III. Turnovsky, Stephen J.
HD75.E2615   2004
338.9 – dc22   2003061674

ISBN 0 521 83561 5 hardback

Contents

Preface

Economic growth continues to be one of the most active areas in macroeconomics. Early contributions by Robert Solow (*Quarterly Journal of Economics*, 1956) and Trevor Swan (*Economic Record*, 1956) laid the foundations for the research that was conducted during the next 15 years or so. Intense research activity continued until the early 1970s, when, because of inflation and oil shocks, interests in macroeconomics were redirected to issues pertaining to short-run macroeconomic stabilization policies. Interest in growth theory was rekindled in 1986 with the contribution by Paul Romer (*Journal of Political Economy*, 1986) and the development of the so-called endogenous growth model. In contrast to the earlier models in which the steady-state growth rate was tied to the population growth rate and, thus, was essentially exogenous, the long-run growth emerged as an equilibrium outcome, reflecting the behavior of the optimizing agents in the economy. Research in growth theory is continuing and is now much more broadly based than the earlier literature of the 1960s.

This book brings together a number of contributions in growth theory and macroeconomic dynamics that reflect these more recent developments and ongoing debates over the relative merits of neoclassical and endogenous growth models. In so doing, we focus on three areas that have received attention recently. First, we develop a number of growth models that extend the theory in different directions. Second, one concern of the recent literature in growth and dynamics is on the statistical properties of the underlying data and on trying to ensure that the growth models are consistent with the empirical evidence. Third, macrodynamics and growth theory has focused increasingly on international aspects, no doubt a reflection in part of the increasing integration of the world economy.

The idea for this book was stimulated in part by the writings of John Pitchford, an emeritus professor at the Australian National University (ANU), who has worked extensively in the general area of macrodynamics over the past 40 years, making many seminal contributions. Perhaps most notable is the fact that his 1960 paper published in the *Economic Record* was in fact the first published formulation and analysis of the constant elasticity of substitution (CES) production function, which of course has been a central relationship in both theoretical and quantitative macroeconomics since then. Most people are unaware that the Pitchford paper actually predates the Arrow, Chenery, Minhas, and Solow paper (*Review of Economics and Statistics*, 1961), but that is in fact the case. In his paper, Pitchford also demonstrated that, for a high elasticity of substitution, the equilibrium in his model might involve ongoing growth, making it an early (but not the earliest) example of an endogenous growth model as well. Pitchford also made important contributions, of both a theoretical and statistical nature, in international macroeconomics, including work on the current account. Thus, the purpose of this book is to bring together high-level contemporary contributions in some (but not all) of the areas of macrodynamics with which Pitchford himself is associated.

It will be apparent to readers of this volume that it has a distinctly "Australian" and, more specifically, "ANU" flavor. Indeed, Trevor Swan himself wrote his seminal paper at the ANU, whereas Pitchford's 1960 paper was written during the period he was at the University of Melbourne, shortly before he joined the ANU. In fact, the ANU has a strong tradition in macroeconomic dynamics in which John Pitchford has played a pivotal role. Back in 1977, he and Stephen Turnovsky edited a collection of ANU papers titled *Applications of Control Theory to Economic Analysis* and published by North-Holland. This was one of the first comprehensive sets of papers in the area and had some influence in this growing area over the subsequent years. Accordingly, in selecting the papers, and in part to honor this tradition spearheaded by Pitchford, most (but not all) of the authors have some Australian, and in particular some ANU connection, either as former students, colleagues, or visitors. We view this as significant, since

Australia, being a small open economy, offers its own challenging problems to issues in macroeconomic dynamics and growth.

The book comprises eight chapters dealing with the following topics.

PART ONE: TOPICS IN GROWTH THEORY

The book begins by reprinting John Pitchford's seminal paper on the CES production, which was originally published in the *Economic Record* in 1960. In addition to exploring its properties, this paper also shows how for values of the elasticity of substitution greater than one capital accumulation is capable of generating long-run endogenous growth. Thus, in addition to pioneering the CES production function, it is also one of the first endogenous growth models as well.

Chapter 2 by Long and Shimomura investigates an old idea that has not received the attention it deserves in economics, which is the proposition that people are concerned with their relative rather than their absolute well-being. Recently, a number of papers have been written under the rubric of "keeping up with the Joneses," "habit formation," and "time-dependent utility." According to this literature, agents' utility depends on their relative, as well as their absolute, level of consumption. Long and Shimomura apply this to wealth, rather than consumption, investigating its implications for the dynamics of both the standard neoclassical growth models and endogenous growth models. They consider the possibility that individuals may desire to increase their wealth not just for its own sake but to improve their standing relative to others, investigating the consequences for inequality and growth. Concern for relative wealth induces a "Rat Race": everybody tries harder because everyone else is trying harder, increasing the level of saving, investment, and growth above the social optimum. Wealth consciousness also tends to reduce inequality over time – the relatively poor have a greater incentive to improve their position than the rich have to maintain their position. The authors find sufficient conditions for these tendencies to hold.

Aghion, García-Peñalosa, and Howitt take a different view of the process driving growth. Rather than relying on the accumulation of physical capital, they argue that growth is fueled by investment in research and development, producing innovative products and processes.

The paper responds to the challenge of the 1990s neoclassical counter-revolution by showing that adaptations to the simple Schumpeterian model of endogenous growth do allow it to explain features such as conditional convergence among "clubs" of countries, once allowance is made for technological spillovers between countries. Countries that invest in human capital and research are able to take advantage of ideas developed in other countries. An innovative aspect of the paper is the distinction the authors draw between "creating knowledge" and "absorbing knowledge." With regard to the first issue, the authors show how the Schumpeterian framework can yield insights on the impact of institutions, legislation, and policy on the rate of knowledge creation and, thus, on the growth rate of productivity. The second topic pertains to the transmission of knowledge across countries and its consequences for cross-country convergence.

PART TWO: STATISTICAL ISSUES IN ECONOMIC GROWTH AND DYNAMICS

Chapter 4 by Dowrick is also concerned with the dynamics of economic growth. The focus here is on the method used to approximate the growth dynamics of the neoclassical growth model in order to estimate the speed of convergence to steady state. A celebrated paper by Mankiw, Romer, and Weil (*Quarterly Journal of Economics*, 1992) takes a first-order approximation to the growth dynamics and estimates rates of convergence for a cross section of 97 countries. Dowrick demonstrates that these estimates underestimate the true rate of convergence because of errors in specifying the linearized dynamics. He provides corrected estimates based on nonlinear estimation techniques.

Barnett and He look at the bifurcation of parameter spaces in macroeconomic models. They identify the presence of what they call singularity bifurcation and compare it to other more familiar forms of bifurcation, such as the Hopf bifurcations. Bifurcation in general is important in understanding the dynamics of modern, macromodels, and singularity bifurcation, although known in engineering, is less familiar to economists. Barnett and He emphasize its potential importance to economics, particularly with the increased usage of Euler equations and in the estimation of their underlying "deep" parameters.

PART THREE: DYNAMIC ISSUES IN INTERNATIONAL ECONOMICS

In Chapter 6, Fisher and Vousden develop an n country model, with each levying its own tariff, capital flowing freely across international borders, but wherein labor is a fixed factor in each country. It contrasts static trade creation, an increase in the volume of trade at a fixed growth rate, with dynamic trade creation, which arises if the change in the growth rate raises the volume of trade. The paper shows that the introduction of a tariff creates net trade if and only if it raises the growth rate of the world economy. The authors also establish that the growth effects of customs unions and free trade areas depend on whether their member countries are sources or hosts of foreign investment.

Chatterjee and Turnovsky explore the implications of tying foreign aid to public investment, an important issue motivated by recent conditions imposed by the European Union on potential member nations. The analysis uses the framework of an endogenous growth model in which both public and private capital are productive factors. The model allows for installation costs and for varying degrees of substitutability between public and private capital, employing for this purpose the CES production function. The paper demonstrates that the benefit of tying aid to public investment is crucially dependent on the elasticity of substitution and the magnitude of installation costs. It has important public policy implications, suggesting that tied aid may be particularly appropriate for less-developed economies, where the elasticity of substitution between public and private capital is typically low.

The final paper by Jones discusses an important issue in aggregation, emphasizing how smooth aggregate data may disguise what he calls churning behavior at the microlevel, whereby some sectors are growing at, say, 40% a year while others are declining at the same rate. The paper considers a pair of examples of this phenomenon in an open economy, one focused on international trade and the other on technology. The analysis shows how some of the current leaders may become the next period's followers in a world in which there is technological progress, despite the existence of perfect foresight and no myopia.

Overall, we view these eight papers as providing a cohesive set of contributions in three intersecting areas of modern macrodynamics, encompassing the theoretical aspects, particularly of growth, and the numerical and statistical aspects, as well as dealing with some international issues. In focusing on these topics we feel that it is a reflection of modern macrodynamics, in general, and growth theory, in particular. At the same time, by linking the material back to some of the early work on production theory and growth, we are reminding ourselves of the origins of some of our current work, something that is all too often forgotten. One final note: Neil Vousden, the coauthor of Chapter 6, was John Pitchford's first Ph.D. student and subsequent colleague at the ANU. Neil was an outstanding economist and an important contributor to the literature on trade protection, among other fields. Regrettably, he passed away in December 2000 at an all-too-early age.

Contributors

Philippe Aghion
Department of Economics
University College London
London, United Kingdom
and
Department of Economics
Harvard University
Cambridge, Massachusetts

William Barnett
Department of Economics
University of Kansas
Lawrence, Kansas

Santanu Chatterjee
Department of Economics
University of Georgia
Athens, Georgia

Steve Dowrick
Department of Economics, School of Economics
Australian National University
Canberra, Australia

Eric Fisher
Department of Economics
Ohio State University
Columbus, Ohio

Cecilia García-Peñalosa
GREQAM
Université Aix-Marseille III
Marseille, France

Yijun He
Department of Economics
Washington State University
Pullman, Washington

Peter Howitt
Department of Economics
Brown University
Providence, Rhode Island

Ronald W. Jones
Department of Economics
University of Rochester
Rochester, New York

Ngo Van Long
Department of Economics
McGill University
Montreal, Quebec, Canada

John D. Pitchford
Department of Economics
Research School of Social Sciences
Australian National University
Canberra, Australia

Rohan Pitchford
Asia Pacific School of Economics and Management
Australian National University
Canberra, Australia

Koji Shimomura
RIEB
Kobe University
Kobe, Japan

Stephen Turnovsky
Department of Economics
University of Washington
Seattle, Washington

Neil Vousden (now deceased)
Australian National University
Canberra, Australia

PART ONE

Topics in Growth Theory

1

Growth and the Elasticity of Factor Substitution

John D. Pitchford

One measure of the shape of production isoquants is the elasticity of substitution between factors. It ranges in value from zero to infinity, implying that no substitution is possible when it is zero and that factors are perfect substitutes when it is infinity. It has been a limitation on the generality of the conclusions of growth models that explicit treatment of substitution has largely been confined to cases in which the elasticity of substitution between labor and capital is unity. This limitation is imposed by the use of the Cobb–Douglas production function.[1] This chapter is based on Professor Swan's growth model, but the Cobb–Douglas production function is replaced by a production function which allows the elasticity of substitution to take any value between zero and infinity. It is seen that a variety of growth paths is possible, depending on the elasticity of substitution, and this leads to a reconsideration of the relation between income growth and the saving ratio.

---

[1] Solow, *op. cit.*, does consider the case in which the elasticity of substitution is 2. T. W. Swan's model, "Economic Growth and Capital Accumulation," *Economic Record*, 1956, uses the Cobb–Douglas function.

The development of this article has benefited from discussions with B. Thalberg and T. N. Srinivasan at Yale, and K. Frearson of the University of Melbourne. I am also indebted to Professor T. W. Swan and Dr. I. F. Pearce of the Australian National University and Professor R. M. Solow of the Massachusetts Institute of Technology, who made useful comments on an earlier draft. The production function I have used was employed by R. M. Solow in a talk at Yale titled "Substitution between Capital and Labour." Professor Solow discussed this function in connection with procedures for estimating the elasticity of substitution. A similar function appears in his article, "A Contribution to the Theory of Economic Growth," *Quarterly Journal of Economics*, 1956, p. 77.

I

Because the model differs from Swan's only in the substitution possibilities which it allows I shall not explain in detail the meaning of the
system.[2]

Symbols

Y–income; $y = \dfrac{dY}{dt} \cdot \dfrac{1}{Y}$;

K–capital; $k = \dfrac{dK}{dt} \cdot \dfrac{1}{K}$;

N–labor; $n = \dfrac{dN}{dt} \cdot \dfrac{1}{N}$;

σ–the elasticity of substitution between capital and labor
s–the average *equals* the marginal saving ratio.

Savings are assumed equal to investment and the marginal product
of labor equal to the real wage throughout.
   The first assumption gives

$$\frac{dK}{dt} \cdot \frac{1}{K} = k = sY/K. \tag{1}$$

The second ensures that labor offering for employment is always
equal to the demand for labor.
   The production function is

$$Y = \left[\gamma K^{-\beta} + \mu N^{-\beta} \right]^{-\frac{1}{\beta}}, \tag{2}$$

where $\beta = (1 - \sigma)/\sigma$,[3] $\gamma = j(\beta)$, and $\mu = h(\beta)$ so that when $\beta = 0$,
$\gamma + \mu = 1$. It is necessary to impose this restriction on the values of
γ and μ when $\beta = 0$ (i.e., $\sigma = 1$) in order to ensure that for all values
of β the function exhibits constant returns to scale. This is ensured for
values of β other than zero by raising $(\gamma K^{-\beta} + \mu N^{-\beta})$ to the power
$-1/\beta$.
   This function then has the elasticity of substitution as a parameter,
for σ may be given any value from zero to infinity by letting β take an
appropriate value in the range of infinity to minus unity.

---

[2] The limitations which his simplifying assumptions produce apply also to my model.
[3] Thus, when $0 < \sigma < 1, \infty > \beta > 0$; and when $0 < \sigma < \infty, 0 > \beta > -1$.

For any differentiable function $Y = f(K, N)$, where Y, N, and K are functions of t, we may write

$$\frac{dY}{dt} = \frac{\partial Y}{\partial K} \cdot \frac{dK}{dt} + \frac{\partial Y}{\partial N} \cdot \frac{dN}{dt},$$

and, hence,

$$\frac{dY}{dt}\frac{1}{Y} = \frac{\partial Y}{\partial K}\frac{K}{Y} \cdot \frac{dK}{dt}\frac{1}{K} + \frac{\partial Y}{\partial N}\frac{N}{Y} \cdot \frac{dN}{dt}\frac{1}{N}$$

or $y = \epsilon_k k + \epsilon_N n$, where ϵ_K and ϵ_N are the production elasticities of capital and labor, respectively.

From (2) we have

$$\epsilon_K = \gamma \left(\frac{Y}{K}\right)^{\beta},$$

and

$$\epsilon_N = \mu \left(\frac{Y}{N}\right)^{\beta}.$$

Thus, in terms of the rates of growth of product and factors, (2) may be written

$$y = \gamma \left(\frac{Y}{K}\right)^{\beta} k + \mu \left(\frac{Y}{N}\right)^{\beta} n. \tag{3}$$

Because we are assuming constant returns to scale, we must also have

$$y = \gamma \left(\frac{Y}{K}\right)^{\beta} k + \left[1 - \gamma \left(\frac{Y}{K}\right)^{\beta}\right] n. \tag{4}$$

Swan's model is depicted on a diagram with growth rates on the vertical and the output–capital ratio on the horizontal axis. On this diagram the labor force growth rate (assumed constant) appears as a horizontal straight line, while the capital growth rate ($k = s(Y/K)$) is a straight line through the origin with slope s. The output growth line completes the system. In the Swan model it is given by $y = \epsilon_K k + (1 - \epsilon_K) n$, where ϵ_K and $1 - \epsilon_K$ are the *constant* production elasticities attached to capital and labor, respectively.

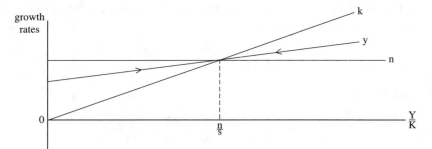

Figure 1. Swan Diagram.

It follows from (3) that when $\sigma = 1$ $(\beta = 0)$, Swan's solution emerges as a special case for

$$y = \gamma \left(\frac{Y}{K}\right)^0 k + \mu \left(\frac{Y}{N}\right)^0 n$$
$$\therefore y = \gamma k + \mu n.$$

This system is shown in Figure 1. A stable (*golden age*) equilibrium is seen to exist when $y = k = n$, and $Y/K = n/s$. This equilibrium will involve the same rate of growth of income whatever the saving ratio. Moreover, as (during the process of adjustment from one equilibrium to another) "'plausible' figuring suggests that even the impact effect of a sharp rise in the saving ratio may be of minor importance for the rate of growth"[4] saving is seen to be unimportant as an influence on the income growth rate.

We should not, however, be misled into ignoring the effect which an increase in the saving ratio will have on the *level*, as distinct from the equilibrium *rate of growth*, of income. A rise in the saving ratio increases output per head and, hence, raises the base upon which income grows.[5]

II

Let us now allow for the full range of possible values of the elasticity of substitution by employing the production function given by Equation

[4] Swan, *op. cit.*, p. 338.
[5] *Ibid*. For the Cobb–Douglas production function it may be shown that $Y/K = (Y/N)^{(\epsilon_K/\epsilon_N)}$, from which the preceding results follow.

$(2).$[6] This function is found to operate only for a limited range of the values of Y/K. Rearranging (2), we have

$$\frac{Y}{K} = \left[\gamma + \mu \left(\frac{K}{N} \right)^{\beta} \right]^{-\frac{1}{\beta}}.$$

Now when the elasticity of substitution is greater than unity $(\beta < 0)$ the output–capital ratio is seen to have a lower limit, $(1/\gamma)^{\frac{1}{\beta}}$, because any value of Y/K below this would require a capital–labor ratio greater than infinity. Thus at the limiting value of Y/K the capital–labor ratio would have to be infinite. When the elasticity of substitution is less than unity $(\beta > 0)$ there is an upper limit to Y/K of $\left(\frac{1}{\gamma}\right)^{\frac{1}{\beta}}$, and at this upper limit it can be seen that the capital–labor ratio will be zero.

These limiting values of the output–capital ratio are shown in the following diagrams. Figures 2(a), 2(b), 2(c), and 2(d) illustrate the growth paths which the model may take; the shape of the income growth line being based on propositions which are obtained in the Appendix.

If the elasticity of substitution is less than unity, Figures 2(a) and 2(b) will be relevant, whilst Figures 2(c) and 2(d) apply to cases in which the elasticity of substitution is greater than unity. If $\sigma < 1$, Figure 2(a) is more likely than Figure 2(b), the higher the output–capital ratio appropriate to a golden age (n/s), and the lower the limiting value of the output–capital ratio $[(1/\gamma)^{\frac{1}{\beta}}]$. $(Y/K) = n/s$ will be higher the greater the population growth rate and the lower the saving ratio. If the population growth rate is higher than the saving ratio $(n/s > 1)$, $(1/\gamma)^{\frac{1}{\beta}}$ must also be greater than unity in order for Figure 2(b) to be applicable. β in this case is positive, so that in order for $(1/\gamma)^{\frac{1}{\beta}}$ to be greater than unity γ must be smaller than unity. On the other hand, if $n/s < 1$, a value of γ smaller than unity will not be necessary to make Figure 2(b) relevant.

If $\sigma > 1$, Figure 2(d) is more likely than Figure 2(c) the lower n/s, and the higher $(1/\gamma)^{\frac{1}{\beta}}$. Thus, the greater the saving ratio and the smaller the rate of population growth the more probable will be

---

[6] The case in which $\sigma = 0$, $\beta = \infty$ is not explicitly treated in what follows. When there is no substitution between factors we have the elements of the simplified Harrod and Joan Robinson models. There is an excellent treatment of the Harrod case in the literature (Solow, *op. cit.*). When $\sigma = \infty$, $\beta = -1$, the production function reduces to $Y = \gamma K + \mu N$, which may be rewritten $y = \gamma (K/Y)k + \mu (N/Y)n$, and yields the same sorts of results as the more general form.

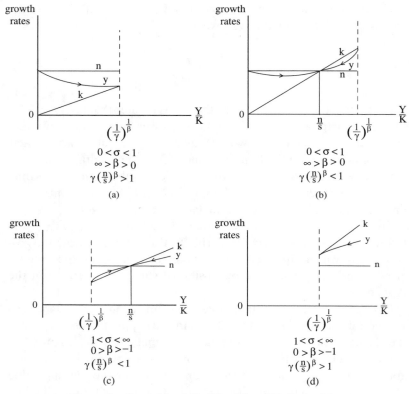

Figure 2. Growth and the Elasticity of Substitution.

Figure 2(d). If $n/s > 1$, $(1/\gamma)^{\frac{1}{\beta}}$ must be greater than unity. This would require (with $\beta < 0$) a value of γ greater than unity. With $n/s < 1$, γ need not be greater than unity in order to ensure that Figure 2(d) applies.

Our knowledge of the values of some of these parameters does not help us to make a choice between these four cases. We know that usually $n < s$, but we do not know anything about the value of γ, nor about the value of σ (unless we take the fitting of Cobb–Douglas production functions to suggest that it is in the neighborhood of unity). Even if we did know the value of σ it would still be necessary to know γ before we could choose between Figures 2(a) and 2(b) ($\sigma < 1$) and between Figures 2(c) and 2(d) ($\sigma > 1$).

Before we examine each of these behavior paths it is useful to look at some of the elementary propositions about growth with constant returns to scale.[7]

We have that

$$y = (1 - \epsilon_N)k + \epsilon_N n$$

for a production function subject to constant returns to scale;

$$\therefore y - k = \epsilon_N n - \epsilon_N k$$

$$= \epsilon_N s \left(\frac{n}{s} - \frac{Y}{K} \right). \tag{5}$$

Given $\epsilon_N > 0$, this system is seen to be stable and to approach a (golden age) equilibrium in which $Y/K = n/s$ or $y = k = n$.

Thus, provided $\epsilon_N > 0$, a golden age is always approached when there are constant returns to scale and no technical progress.

This suggests the basis of distinction between the two different types of behavior which the model can produce. In those cases in which the system grows towards a golden age (Figures 2(b) and 2(c)) the labor production elasticity (ϵ_N) must be positive throughout the process, whereas if a golden age is not approached forces must be in operation to push the labor elasticity to (a limiting position of) zero.

The two golden age cases do not require much explanation, for the shifts in the production elasticities and the marginal productivities which bring the system to equilibrium may be inferred from a consideration of the diagrams and Equations (3) and (4). These cases, of course, obey the rule that the income growth rate is, in equilibrium, uninfluenced by the saving ratio. It is the two cases in which a golden age is not possible that invite detailed examination.

As we have seen in both these cases the contribution of labor to the productive process eventually becomes negligible in the sense that, after a point, further increases in the labor force employed fail to increase output significantly. Figure 2(a) ($\sigma < 1$) involves the labor force growing more rapidly than the capital stock. Because the capital–labor ratio is continually falling, labor must be increasingly substituted for capital in order to maintain full employment of both factors. The fact that labor and capital are poor substitutes will mean that more and

---

[7] See T. W. Swan, "Golden Ages and Production Functions," in K. E. Berrill (ed.), *Economic Development with Special Reference to East Asia*, London; MacMillan, 1963.

more labor can be employed only if the real wage (*equals* the marginal product of labor) is forced down. In this case the marginal product of labor falls more rapidly than output per head (i.e., $\partial Y/\partial N$ falls more rapidly than N/Y rises) so that the labor production elasticity, $(\partial Y/\partial N) \cdot (N/Y) = \mu(Y/N)^\beta$, declines. Before a golden age can be reached the capital–labour ratio has tended to zero so that the fall in the capital–output ratio comes to a halt. It follows that if, in equilibrium, the labor elasticity is zero, output (with constant returns to scale) must grow at the same rate as capital. Hence, as capital grows more slowly than labor, output must grow at a less than golden age rate. Of course this equilibrium will be reached only after infinite time has elapsed, but it can be stated that in the circumstances in which Figure 2(a) holds income will grow towards such an equilibrium, and during this process the income growth rate will always be less than the labor growth rate.

The decline in the marginal product of labor implies a fall in the real wage. Before real wages fall to zero the labor force growth rate will decline (either because population growth is reduced by a Malthusian process, or because unemployment develops). As long as some accumulation is taking place the result will be eventually to render a golden age possible (i.e., to ensure $\gamma(n/s)^\beta < 1$). However, as the labor growth rate has fallen the income growth rate will be less than the initial labor growth rate and there may be some unemployed labor at the new equilibrium.

Figure 2(d) ($\sigma > 1$) involves income growing permanently at a higher rate than labor. This causes a rise in the capital–output ratio; for when income grows faster than employment, with constant returns to scale, capital must be growing more rapidly than income. This deepening of capital would eventually produce a golden age, except that in this case the capital–labour ratio becomes infinite before such an equilibrium can be reached. Capital and labor are good substitutes in this situation, and capital is increasingly substituted for labor as the process proceeds. The marginal product of labor is raised by this substitution, but, nevertheless, as in the previous case, the labor elasticity (ϵ_N) tends to zero as the limiting value of the output–capital ratio is approached.

This case is associated with a high saving ratio and/or a low population growth and a high value of the constant attached to capital (γ). The labor production elasticity must eventually fall to zero because the community eventually has such a large stock of capital compared

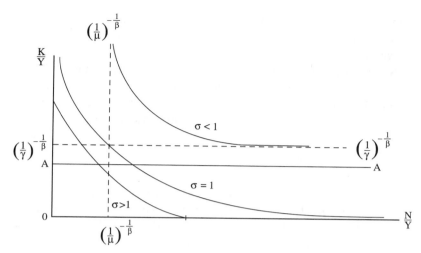

Figure 3. Isoquants.

to the stock of labor, and this capital is a good substitute for labor, so that a given percentage change in the labor force produces a negligible percentage change in the level of output.

All this can be looked at in terms of the shape and position of the production isoquants for different values of the elasticity of substitution. The production Function (2) may be stated in the form of a relationship between K/Y and N/Y. Thus,

$$\frac{K}{Y} = \left[\frac{1}{\gamma} - \frac{\mu}{\gamma} \left(\frac{N}{Y} \right)^{-\beta} \right]^{-\frac{1}{\beta}}. \tag{6}$$

In the Appendix it is shown that this relationship will involve the forms shown in Figure 3 for different values of σ.

For any given level of income these curves illustrate the possible shapes of the production isoquants. When $\sigma > 1$, (6) will be asymptotic to positive limits with respect to both K/Y and N/Y. When $\sigma = 1$, (6) will be asymptotic to both axes, whilst when $\sigma > 1$, (6) will cut both axes at finite values.

Now in a golden age $k = s(Y/K) = n$, so that for an economy to attain a golden age it must attain a capital–output ratio such that $K/Y = s/n$. The line AA in Figure 3 is one such equilibrium value of K/Y. It is clear that the Cobb–Douglas production function can attain any capital–output ratio, so that, from any initial value, growth will take place along the curve for $\sigma = 1$ until the appropriate value of K/Y is reached. On the other hand, if $\sigma \neq 1$, it can be seen that only if the line AA cuts Equation (6) will a golden age be possible. In Figure 3, AA is drawn so that with the curve given for $\sigma > 1$ a golden age can be reached, but in the case of the curve for $\sigma < 1$ a movement downward and to the right can never attain the required value of s/n.

III

One interesting implication of these processes is that in some circumstances a rise in the saving ratio can achieve a permanently higher rate of growth of income. Swan had concluded that "[A]fter a transitional phase, the influence of the saving ratio on the rate of growth is ultimately absorbed by a compensating change in the output–capital ratio."[8] However, he had not examined the possibility of the labor elasticity becoming zero and, thus, had not allowed for cases such as Figures 2(a) and 2(d).

Only when substitution is difficult and a golden age is achievable will it be impossible permanently to raise the rate of growth of income by raising the saving ratio.[9] As we have seen, when substitution is difficult and a golden age is not possible, income will aways grow at a rate less than the golden age growth rate. An appropriate rise in the saving ratio (provided this can be achieved) will make a golden age possible so that income can eventually grow at the same rate as labor.

In a golden age, when substitution is easy, a higher income growth rate may be produced by raising the saving ratio. This means that the higher saving changes the process from the type shown by Figure 2(c) to the type shown by Figure 2(d).

Apart from the possibility of shifting from one diagram to another it is possible in Figures 2(a) and 2(d) to raise the *equilibrium* growth rate by raising the saving ratio. Raising s does not influence the value of $(\frac{1}{\gamma})^{\frac{1}{\beta}}$ (the limit to the values of Y/K), so that as the slope of the k line rises its intersection with the vertical produced from $(\frac{1}{\gamma})^{\frac{1}{\beta}}$ describes the locus of higher and higher equilibria.

---

[8] "Economic Growth and Capital Accumulation," p. 338.
[9] $\sigma = 1$ is taken to separate "difficult" from "easy" substitution.

It is worthwhile noting that in some cases "plausible" changes in the saving ratio can induce significant changes in equilibrium income growth.

But it is not only equilibrium that matters. In all such processes as these, equilibrium is never literally reached, and when, in equilibrium, some variable such as the capital–labor ratio has to become zero or infinite, it is reasonable to assume that the system will usually take a very long time to get near to equilibrium. In such cases comparisons of equilibrium situations are not particularly useful. However, in the case of Figure 2(d), knowledge of the equilibrium income growth rate does prove useful because it turns out to be the lowest possible income growth rate under those conditions. This can be seen if we substitute (1) in (4) and differentiate y with respect to Y/K.

Then we have

$$\frac{dy}{d(Y/K)} = \gamma s(\beta + 1)\left(\frac{Y}{K}\right) - \gamma n\beta \left(\frac{Y}{K}\right)^{\beta - 1},$$

which is positive when $\sigma > 1$ $(0 > \beta > -1)$. Hence, y is a monotonically increasing function whose slope is a direct function of s, and the equilibrium income growth rate $y = s(1/\gamma)^{\frac{1}{\beta}}$ is thus the lowest income growth rate which it can attain. Our conclusions about raising the saving ratio then apply *a fortiori* to Figure 2(d).

We are not so fortunate in the case of Figure 2(a), for the function y may or may not have a minimum in the range of attainable values of Y/K. This makes it difficult to offer a general statement about the equilibrium as compared with the nonequilibrium growth rates of income. One would need information about the time path of income in order to be satisfied that a given change in s would make a significant improvement.

Several (rather obvious) qualifications are in order. In the first place, raising the saving ratio may be impossible (without lowering population growth) because no investible surplus above subsistence consumption may exist. Second, it may be very difficult to maintain some of these growth processes and at the same time maintain full employment. In particular the marginal product of capital must become fairly low in Figure 2(d) as the capital–labor ratio gets nearer and nearer to infinity and entrepreneurs' enthusiasm for investment would undoubtedly dwindle. In Figure 2(a) the marginal product of labor tends to zero, in which case pressure for a higher real wage could well interfere with full employment of labor.

APPENDIX

(a) To show that the elasticity of substitution (σ) is a parameter of the production function,

$$Y = \left[\gamma K^{-\beta} + \mu N^{-\beta}\right]^{-\frac{1}{\beta}} \tag{A1}$$

such that $\sigma = 1/(1 + \beta)$.

Now

$$\sigma = \frac{(\partial Y/\partial K) \cdot (\partial Y/\partial N)}{Y \cdot (\partial^2 Y/\partial K \partial N)} \tag{A2}$$

when the production function is linear and homogeneous.[10]

$$\frac{\partial Y}{\partial N} = \mu \left(\frac{Y}{N}\right)^{\beta+1}$$

$$\frac{\partial Y}{\partial K} = \gamma \left(\frac{Y}{K}\right)^{\beta+1}$$

$$Y \cdot \frac{\partial^2 Y}{\partial K \partial N} = (\beta+1)\gamma \left(\frac{Y}{K}\right)^{\beta+1} \mu \left(\frac{Y}{N}\right)^{\beta+1}.$$

Hence, substituting in (A2) we have

$$\sigma = \frac{1}{1+\beta}.$$

(b) The roots of $y - k = \gamma\left(\frac{Y}{K}\right)^{\beta} k + (1 - \gamma\left(\frac{Y}{K}\right)^{\beta})n - k$ will be equilibrium solutions of the system provided they lie within the limits with respect to Y/K imposed by the function. Now $y - k = (k - n)[\gamma (Y/K)^{\beta} - 1]$; thus, $y = k$ when either $k = n$ or $\gamma (Y/K)^{\beta} = 1$.

---

[10] See R. G. D. Allen, *Mathematical Analysis for Economists*, p. 343.

The equilibrium concerned will be stable provided that

$$\frac{dy}{d\left(\frac{Y}{K}\right)} < \frac{dk}{d\left(\frac{Y}{K}\right)} = s.$$

Now

$$\frac{dy}{d(Y/K)} = (\beta + 1)\gamma s \left(\frac{Y}{K}\right)^{\beta} - \beta\gamma n \left(\frac{Y}{K}\right)^{\beta-1}.$$

If $y = k = n$, $Y/K = n/s$,

$$\frac{dy}{d(Y/K)} = \gamma n^{\beta} s^{1-\beta},$$

which is stable if $\gamma n^{\beta} s^{1-\beta} < s$ or $\gamma(n/s)^{\beta} < 1$. That is, if the golden age falls within achievable values of the output–capital coefficient, it will be stable.

Again if $Y/K = \left(\frac{1}{\gamma}\right)^{\frac{1}{\beta}}$

$$\frac{dy}{d(Y/K)} = s(\beta + 1) - \beta n(\gamma)^{\frac{1}{\beta}}.$$

Thus, this equilibrium is stable if

$$\gamma\left(\frac{n}{s}\right)^{\frac{1}{\beta}} > 1,$$

that is, if it exists.

(c) As $Y/K \to 0$, $y \to n$ if $\beta > 0$.

This can be seen if $Y/K = 0$ is substituted in

$$y = \gamma s \left(\frac{Y}{K}\right)^{\beta+1} + \left(1 - \gamma\left(\frac{Y}{K}\right)^{\beta}\right) n.$$

(d) The propositions contained in (b) and (c) help toward the construction of Figures 2(a), 2(b), 2(c), and 2(d). It remains to show where the y line lies in relation to the k and n lines.

Write

$$y - k = (k - n)\left[\gamma\left(\frac{Y}{K}\right)^{\beta} - 1\right],$$

and

$$y - n = (k - n)\gamma \left(\frac{Y}{K}\right)^{\beta}.$$

If $\gamma (Y/K)^{\beta} < 1$, that is, $Y/K < (1/\gamma)^{\frac{1}{\beta}}$ if $\beta > 0$ and $Y/K > (1/\gamma)^{\frac{1}{\beta}}$ if $\beta < 0$,
when

$$k < n, \ y > k, \ y < n$$
$$k > n, \ y < k, \ y > n.$$

(e) The shape of the function

$$\frac{K}{Y} = \left[\frac{1}{\gamma} - \frac{\mu}{\gamma}\left(\frac{N}{Y}\right)^{-\beta}\right]^{-\frac{1}{\beta}} \tag{A3}$$

$$\frac{d\,(K/Y)}{d\,(N/Y)} = \frac{-(\mu/\gamma)(N/Y)^{-(\beta+1)} \cdot (K/Y)}{(1/\gamma) - (\mu/\gamma)(N/Y)^{-\beta}} \tag{A4}$$

$$= -\frac{\mu}{\gamma}\left(\frac{K}{N}\right)^{\beta+1}$$

$$\frac{d^2\,(K/Y)}{d\,(N/Y)^2} \cdot \frac{1}{[d\,(K/Y)/d\,(N/Y)]} = \frac{d\,(K/Y)}{d\,(N/Y)} \cdot \frac{1}{(K/Y)}$$

$$-(\beta + 1)\left(\frac{N}{Y}\right)^{-1} - \frac{\beta\,(\mu/\gamma)\,(N/Y)^{-(\beta+1)}}{(1/\gamma) - (\mu/\gamma)(N/Y)^{-\beta}}, \tag{A5}$$

(A4) and (A5) are negative so that $d^2\,(K/Y)/d\,(N/Y)^2$ is positive.

Function (A5) thus has a negative slope and is convex to the origin.

When $\sigma > 1$ and $N/Y = 0$, $K/Y = (1/\gamma)^{-\frac{1}{\beta}}$; and when $\sigma > 1$ and $K/Y = 0$, $N/Y = (1/\mu)^{-\frac{1}{\beta}}$.

When $\sigma < 1$ and $N/Y = \infty$, $K/Y = \left(\frac{1}{\gamma}\right)^{-\frac{1}{\beta}}$; and when $\sigma < 1$ and $K/Y = \infty$, $N/Y = (1/\mu)^{-\frac{1}{\beta}}$.

The Cobb–Douglas function may be seen to be a special case of (A1) for the case $\sigma = 1$, $\beta = 0$, $\gamma + \mu = 1$.

From (A1) (appendix)

$$\log Y = \frac{-\log\left[\gamma K^{-\beta} + \mu N^{-\beta}\right]}{\beta}$$

$$\operatorname*{Lt.}_{\beta \to 0} \log Y = -\operatorname*{Lt.}_{\beta \to 0} \frac{\dfrac{d}{d\beta} \log\left[\gamma K^{-\beta} + \mu N^{-\beta}\right]}{d(\beta)/d\beta}$$

$$= -\operatorname*{Lt.}_{\beta \to 0} - \frac{\gamma K^{-\beta} \log K - \mu N^{-\beta} \log N}{\gamma K^{-\beta} + \mu N^{-\beta}}$$

$$= \gamma \log K + \mu \log N.$$

Hence,

$$Y = K^{\gamma} N^{\mu}. \tag{A6}$$

Now rearranging we have

$$\frac{K}{Y} = \left(\frac{N}{Y}\right)^{-\frac{\mu}{\gamma}}$$

$$\frac{d\,(K/Y)}{d\,(N/Y)} = -\frac{\mu}{\gamma} \left(\frac{N}{Y}\right)^{-\left(\frac{\mu}{\gamma}+1\right)},$$

which is less than zero, and

$$\frac{d^2\,(K/Y)}{d\,(N/Y)^2} = \left(\frac{\mu}{\gamma}\right)\left(\frac{\mu}{\gamma}+1\right)\left(\frac{N}{Y}\right)^{-\left(\frac{\mu}{\gamma}+2\right)},$$

which is positive.

It can also be seen that this function will be asymptotic to both axes.

2

Relative Wealth, Catching Up, and Economic Growth

Ngo Van Long and Koji Shimomura

We show that, by including relative wealth in the reduced-form utility function, a number of phenomena can be explained, such as differences in growth rates among nations and the catching up achieved by some poor countries, in a world where initial wealths are not equally distributed. We give sufficient conditions for the final distribution of wealth to be independent of the initial distribution, and conditions for saddlepoint stability in a two-class model. The question of catching up was studied by Stiglitz (1969) under the assumption that individuals do not save optimally. Stiglitz showed that if all individuals save a constant fraction of their income, then eventually the poor will catch up with the rich. Kemp and Shimomura (1992) demonstrated that catching up will not occur if individuals save optimally (and care only about their consumption). In this chapter, we show that if individuals care enough about their relative wealth, then catching up will take place under optimal saving.

1. INTRODUCTION

Why do countries grow at different rates? Economists have offered a variety of explanations. One of these is the difference in saving rates. Countries that save a higher fraction of their income accumulate capital faster; this results in higher growth rates of income (at least in the short run). But why do saving rates differ across countries? One possible explanation is that utility discount rates may differ, even if the instantaneous utility functions may be identical. An alternative explanation is that an individual's utility may be a function of several variables, one of which is relative wealth. An individual's concern about

18

his relative position in society may have an influence on his saving behavior.

It is widely acknowledged that it is not wealth *per se* that is wanted; rather wealth (relative wealth) is valued because it gives access to non-market goods such as status and influence. This view was expressed in Adam Smith's "The Theory of Moral Sentiments":

To what purpose is all the toil and bustle of the world? . . . It is our vanity that urges us on. . . . It is not wealth that men desire, but the consideration and good opinion that wait upon riches.[1]

The recognition that non-market goods are arguments in the direct utility function of economic agents leads to a useful formulation: wealth appears in their *reduced-form utility function*. The purpose of this chapter is to demonstrate how such a reduced-form utility function can be used to explain a number of phenomena, such as differences in growth rates, catching up, and so forth.

Influential articles on status-seeking include work by Akerlof (1976), Cole et al. (1992), and Konrad (1992). Akerlof pointed out that status-seeking could result in a "Rat Race," which could well be a pure waste. Cole et al. demonstrated that wealth should appear in a reduced-form utility function. A model with two types of agents was considered by Konrad. He showed that those who care only about their consumption may benefit from the existence of agents who care about relative wealth. Society as a whole may overaccumulate capital.

This chapter contains two new contributions: a study of the role of status-seeking in a model of endogenous growth and an analysis of conditions under which poor individuals (or countries) will be able to catch up with the richer ones.

Our endogenous growth model of the AK type (in Section 4) has the distinctive property that individuals give a weight to their concern about relative wealth. We show that, in a world consisting of closed economies, countries in which individuals give a greater weight to their concern about relative wealth will achieve a higher rate of long-run growth. This analysis provides a possible explanation for differences in long-run growth rates.

---

[1] Quoted by Cole et al. (1992, p. 1092), who also refer to Madonna's famous line, "The boy with the cold hard cash is always Mister Right because we are living in the material world and I am a material girl" (Madonna, "Material Girl").

Concerning catching up, Stiglitz (1969) was the first to investigate this question using a neoclassical aggregate production function (a non-AK technology). Under the assumption that individuals save a constant fraction of their income, he demonstrated that eventually the poor will catch up with the rich. Kemp and Shimomura (1992), however, demonstrated that catching up will not occur if individuals save optimally. In Section 5 of this chapter, assuming a non-AK technology, we show that if individuals care enough about their relative wealth, then catching up will take place under optimal saving. Applying this analysis to a community of trading nations with equalized factor prices (perhaps due to international capital mobility), our model predicts that during the transition phase poorer countries will grow faster than richer ones, with the difference being more pronounced the greater is the weight given to the concern about relative wealth.

Section 2 provides an overview of the universal phenomenon of status-seeking. Section 3 considers a model with identical agents who seek to maximize the value of their discounted stream of utility. It is shown that their concern about their relative wealths leads to more capital accumulation, as compared to the standard Cass–Ramsey model. In Section 4, we introduce status-seeking into in the framework of the AK endogenous growth model, also referred to as the Solow–Pitchford AK model[2] in view of the pioneering work of Solow (1956) and Pitchford (1960), who showed that constant growth in per capita consumption is feasible without technical progress. We show that economies with greater degrees of status consciousness will achieve higher permanent growth rates. In Section 5, we consider a model with two classes of agents: the poor and the rich. (These may be nations or individuals.) We demonstrate that the poor will eventually catch up with the rich if the marginal utility of relative wealth is very high when relative wealth is low.

2. STATUS-SEEKING: AN OVERVIEW

Status-seeking is common in human and animal species. Two major features of social life in many species of animals are territoriality and hierarchies. Hens compete for high positions in the "peck order" (see Dawkins, 1976, pp. 88 and 122):

---

[2] See Long and Wong (1997).

If a batch of hens who have never met before are introduced to each other, there is usually a great deal of fighting. After a time the fighting dies down. . . . It is because each individual "learns her place" relative to each other individual. This is incidentally good for the group as a whole. As an indicator of this it has been noticed that in established groups of hens, where fierce fighting is rare, egg production is higher than in groups of hens whose membership is continually being changed, and in which fights are consequently more frequent (p. 88).

Contests among members of a group take time, and in the long run a hierarchy is established:

Crickets have a general memory of what happened in past fights. A cricket which has recently won a large number of fights become more hawkish. A cricket which has recently had a losing streak becomes more dovish. This was neatly shown by R. D. Alexander. He used a model cricket to beat up real crickets. After this treatment the real crickets became more likely to lose fights against other real crickets. Each cricket can be thought of as constantly updating his own estimate of his fighting ability, relative to that of an average individual in his population. If animals such as crickets . . . are kept together in a closed group for a time, a kind of dominance hierarchy is likely to develop (Dawkins, 1976, pp. 88–89).

Why do individuals in an animal society want high social rank? Wynne-Edwards (1962) sees high social rank as a ticket of entitlement to reproduce.[3] "Instead of fighting directly over females themselves, individuals fight over social status, and then accept that if they do not end up high on the social scale they are not entitled to breed. They restrain themselves where females are directly concerned, though they may try every now and then to win higher status, and therefore could be said to compete *indirectly* over females."[4]

In human societies, an agent's status is "a ranking device that determines how well he or she fares with respect to the allocation of nonmarket goods" (Cole et al., 1992, p. 1093). Examples of nonmarket goods are membership of the board of trustees of a prestigious university, and the types of friends or partners for your children. In the model developed by Cole et al., a couple, by deciding how much to bequeath to their son, can influence the quality of his mate: "Parents

---

[3] For example, in the case of elephant seals, 4% of the male seals accounted for 88% of all the copulations observed (Dawkins, 1976, p. 154).

[4] ". . . according to Wynne-Edwards, populations use formal contests over status and territory as a means of limiting their size slightly below the level at which starvation itself actually takes its toll" (Dawkins, 1976, p. 123).

will be willing to reduce their consumption if it sufficiently increases the quality of their son's mate" (p. 1099).

Status-seeking may result in a Rat Race, with negative welfare effects: if everyone tries to run faster, it is possible that while more effort is expended, the relative ranking may remain unchanged. This principle applies not only for races among individuals of a given species, but also for races between different species. The idea of zero change in success rate has been given the name of the "Red Queen Effect" by American biologist Leigh van Valen (1973). In Lewis Carroll's *Through the Looking-Glass* (1872), the Red Queen seized Alice by hand and dragged her, faster and faster, on a frenzied run, but no matter how fast they ran, they always stayed in the same place. The puzzled Alice said, "Well in *our* country you'd get to somewhere else – if you ran very fast for a long time as we've been doing." To this the Queen replied: "A slow sort of country! Now, *here*, you see, it takes all the running *you* can do, to keep in the same place. If you want to get somewhere else, you must run at least twice as fast as that."

The possible adverse welfare effects of competition have been noted by non-economists as well as economists. The following paragraph from Richard Dawkins's "The Blind Watchmaker" is illuminating:

Why, for instances, are trees in forests so tall? The short answer is that all the other trees are tall, so no one tree can afford not to be. It would be overshadowed if it did.... But if only they were all shorter, if only there could be some sort of trade-union agreement to lower the recognized height of the canopy in forests, all the trees would benefit. They would be competing with each other in the canopy for exactly the same sun light, but they would all have "paid" much smaller growing costs to get into the canopy (p. 184).

3. A MODIFIED CASS–RAMSEY MODEL WITH IDENTICAL STATUS-SEEKING AGENTS

3.1. Assumptions and Notation

We assume that all individuals have the same reduced-form utility function. Labor does not enter the utility function. Each individual inelastically supplies one unit of labor per unit of time. Let c_i denote individual i's consumption, and k_i his wealth (not including human wealth, which is defined as the present value of the stream of future wage income). Let k denote society's per capita wealth. The reduced-form utility function of individual i is assumed to take the separable form

$$U\left(c_i, \frac{k_i}{k}\right) = u(c_i) + \theta v\left(\frac{k_i}{k}\right),$$

where $u(\cdot)$ and $v(\cdot)$ are strictly concave and increasing functions. The parameter $\theta \geq 0$ is the weight given to the concern about relative wealth. If $\theta = 0$, then the model reduces to the standard textbook version of the Cass–Ramsey model, where wealth does not appear in the utility function.

There is a continuum of individuals, represented by the interval $[0, 1]$. Even though, in a symmetric equilibrium, the ratio $z_i \equiv k_i/k$ is unity, individuals can contemplate deviating from this ratio by investing more or less than the average rate of investment in the economy. Individuals are price-takers: they take the paths of wage rate $W(t)$ and rental rate $R(t)$ as given, independent of their actions.

The agregate production function, in per capita form, is $y = f(k)$. In this section, we assume that $f(k)$ has the usual neoclassical properties, and satisfies the Inada conditions:

$$\lim_{k \to 0} f'(k) = \infty \text{ and } \lim_{k \to \infty} f'(k) = 0.$$

Capital depreciates at the rate $\delta \geq 0$.

Let $c(t)$ denote per capita consumption. The stock $k(t)$ evolves according to the differential equation

$$\dot{k}(t) = f(k(t)) - c(t) - \delta k(t).$$

In a competitive equilibrium, the rental rate is given by

$$R(t) = f'(k(t))$$

and the wage rate is

$$W(t) = f(k(t)) - k(t) f'(k(t)).$$

The rate of interest is equal to the rental rate minus the rate of depreciation:

$$r(t) = R(t) - \delta.$$

Individuals have perfect knowledge of the time paths of future factor prices and per capita capital stock. Individual i seeks to maximize the integral of the discounted utility flow:

$$\max_{c_i(t)} \int_0^\infty \left[u(c_i(t)) + \theta v \left(\frac{k_i(t)}{k(t)} \right) \right] e^{-\rho t} dt, \tag{1}$$

where $\rho > 0$ is the utility-discount rate. The maximization is subject to the constraints

$$\dot{k}_i(t) = R(t)k_i(t) + W(t) - c_i(t) - \delta k_i(t) \tag{2}$$

$$k_i(0) = k_{i0} \tag{3}$$

$$\lim_{t \to \infty} k(t) \exp \left[-\int_0^t r(s)ds \right] = 0. \tag{4}$$

3.2. The Benchmark Scenario: The Social Planner's Problem

It is useful to consider first the benchmark case where a social planner solves the problem on behalf on the individuals. Assume all individuals have the same initial stocks: $k_i(0) = K_j(0)$ for all i, j. Because all individuals are identical, the social planner would set $k_i = k$, thus, $v(z_i) = v(1)$, where $z_i \equiv k_i/k$. The problem is simply

$$\max_{c(t)} \int_0^\infty [u(c(t)) + \theta v(1)]e^{-\rho t} dt$$

subject to

$$\dot{k}(t) = f(k(t)) - c(t) - \delta k(t) \tag{5}$$

$$k(0) = k_0 \tag{6}$$

$$k(t) \geq 0.$$

The solution of this problem is well known. The optimal consumption path must satisfy the Euler equation

$$\frac{\dot{c}(t)}{c(t)} = \frac{1}{\sigma(c(t))}[f'(k(t)) - \delta - \rho], \tag{7}$$

where $\sigma(c)$ is the elasticity of marginal utility:

$$\sigma(c) = -\frac{cu''(c)}{u'(c)} > 0.$$

Furthermore, let k_{ss} be the capital stock level that satisfies the modified golden rule:

$$f'(k_{ss}) = \delta + \rho. \qquad (8)$$

Then, as has been shown in the literature, the optimal path $k(t)$ converges to k_{ss}:

$$\lim_{t \to \infty} k(t) = k_{ss}. \qquad (9)$$

The corresponding steady-state consumption is denoted by c_{ss} where

$$c_{ss} = f(k_{ss}) - \delta k_{ss}.$$

It is well known that c_{ss} (called the "modified golden rule" consumption) is smaller than the maximum sustainable consumption $\hat{c}$, which is defined by

$$\hat{c} = \max_{k}[f(k) - \delta k]. \qquad (10)$$

The intuition behind the result that $c_{ss} < \hat{c}$ is that, given that utility is discounted, it is not optimal to try to reach the maximum sustainable consumption level.

The two differential Equations (5) and (7), together with the two boundary Conditions (6) and (9), determine a unique pair of optimal paths $(k(t), c(t))$ which can be represented by a trajectory in the (k, c) plane that converges to the point (k_{ss}, c_{ss}).

The converging trajectory defines a function $c^* = \phi(k)$, which is the optimal control rule in feedback form. If the social planner instructs all individuals to follow this rule (i.e., $c_i = \phi(k_i)$), and if they all obey, the socially optimal solution can be achieved. However, in general, individuals will have an incentive to deviate from this recommended rule, because each will seek to achieve a higher social status by increasing his wealth above the recommended path. This results in a Rat Race, making all individual worse off. This outcome is considered in more detail in the next subsection.

3.3. Individual Optimization

Each individual i takes the time path of society's per capita capital stock as given. (The time paths of factor prices are also taken as given.) Each contemplates the possibility of steering the ratio k_i / k away from unity.

The Hamiltonian for the optimization problem of individual i is

$$H_i = u(c_i) + \theta v[k_i/k] + \psi_i[r(t)k_i(t) + W(t) - c_i(t)].$$

The necessary conditions[5] are

$$\frac{\partial H_i}{\partial c_i} = u'(c_i(t)) - \psi_i(t) = 0 \tag{11}$$

$$\dot{\psi}_i(t) = \rho\psi_i(t) - \frac{\partial H_i}{\partial k_i(t)} = [\rho - r(t)]\psi_i(t) - \frac{\theta}{k(t)}\frac{dv}{dz_i(t)}, \tag{12}$$

where $z_i = k_i/k$, and

$$\dot{k}_i(t) = \frac{\partial H_i}{\partial \psi_i(t)} = r(t)k_i(t) + W(t) - c_i(t). \tag{13}$$

Boundary Conditions (3) and (4) are used.

From Equation (11) we get

$$u''(c_i)\dot{c}_i = \dot{\psi}_i,$$

hence,

$$\frac{c_i u''(c_i)}{u'(c_i)}\frac{\dot{c}_i}{c_i} = \frac{\dot{\psi}_i}{\psi_i} = [\rho - r(t)] - \frac{\theta}{u'(c_i)k}\frac{dv}{dz_i}. \tag{14}$$

Since $r(t) = f'(k) - \delta$, condition (14) yields, for the economy as a whole,

$$\frac{\dot{c}}{c} = \frac{1}{\sigma(c)}\left[f'(k) - \delta - \rho + (\theta/k)\frac{v'(1)}{u'(c)}\right]. \tag{15}$$

It follows that the steady-state capital stock under *perfectly competitive* behavior, denoted by k_p, satisfies the condition

$$f'(k_p) = \delta + \rho - (\theta/k_p)\frac{v'(1)}{u'(c_p)} < \delta + \rho, \tag{16}$$

where c_p satisfies

$$c_p = f(k_p) - \delta k_p.$$

Proposition 2.1: If individuals are wealth conscious (i.e., $\theta > 0$) then, under laissez-faire, the steady-state capital stock k_p is greater than the stock level k_{ss} that the social planner would wish to achieve.

---

[5] For a new proof of the Maximum Principle, see Long and Shimomura (2003).

Corollary 2.1: If individuals are wealth conscious (i.e., $\theta > 0$) and θ is not too great, then (i) the steady-state consumption under laissez-faire exceeds the modified golden rule consumption c_{ss} that the social planner would wish to achieve, and (ii) their steady-state saving rate (defined as $I/\text{GNP} = \delta k_p / f(k_p)$) exceeds the steady-state saving rate $\delta k_{ss} / f(k_{ss})$ under the social planner.

Proof: If θ is positive but not too large, then $k_p < \hat{k} \equiv \arg \max[f(k) - \delta k]$. Now, $f(k) - \delta k$ is an increasing function of k for all $k < \hat{k}$. It follows that $c_p > c_{ss}$. This proves (i). To prove (ii), note that $f(k)/k$ is a decreasing function of k. ∎

Proposition 2.2: If σ is a constant, and $\theta > 0$, then at any stock level $k < k_p$ the rate of consumption *growth*, $\dot{c}/c$, under laissez-faire is greater than the rate of consumption growth under the social planner.

Proof: Compare Equation (15) with Equation (7). ∎

Remark 2.1: Proposition 2.2 implies that initially (at time $t = 0$) individuals under the laissez-faire scenario have a lower consumption level than they would under the social planner. This higher saving rate (in the initial phase) is the outcome of the individual's desire to accumulate wealth k_i so as not to fall behind the forecasted path of society's average wealth $k(t)$. Each individual thinks that all others are trying to run faster than him, and this results in a Rat Race,[6] which ultimately makes everyone worse off (i.e., the value of the integral of discounted utility flow under laissez-faire is lower than the one achieved under the social planner).

4. A MODIFIED ENDOGENOUS GROWTH MODEL

We now turn to an endogenous growth model of the AK variety: the per capita production function is either linear in the capital labor ratio for all $k \geq 0$, or approaches such a linear function as k tends to infinity.[7]

---

[6] See Akerlof (1976) for an insightful discussion of the Rat Race.

[7] For early papers dealing with this second variety of production functions, see Solow (1956) and especially Pitchford (1960), who provided a comprehensive analysis of perpetual growth in per capita consumption without technical progress. Long and Wong (1997) refer to that model as the Solow–Pitchford AK model.

We postulate the production function

$$y = Ak,$$

where

$$A > \rho,$$

that is, the technology is sufficiently productive to overcome the force of discounting. Concerning the utility function, we will consider the following two cases in the next two subsections.

Case 1: The utility function is additively separable:

$$U\left(c_i, \frac{k_i}{k}\right) = u(c_i) + \theta v\left[\frac{k_i}{k}\right] = \ln c_i + \theta \ln\left[\frac{k_i}{k}\right], \quad \theta \geq 0 \qquad (17)$$

Case 2: The utility function is multiplicatively separable:

$$U\left(c_i, \frac{k_i}{k}\right) = \left(\frac{c_i^\alpha}{\alpha}\right)\left[1 + \theta\left(\frac{k_i}{k}\right)^\beta\right], \quad \theta \geq 0, \quad 1 > \beta > 0, \quad 1 > \alpha > 0$$

$$(18)$$

Notice that $\alpha > 0$ ensures that $\partial U / \partial k_i \geq 0$.

We continue to assume that all individuals have identical initial wealths.

4.1. Case 1

4.1.1. The Social Planner's Problem

The social planner seeks to

$$\max_{c(t)} \int_0^\infty [\ln(c(t)) + \theta \ln(1)] e^{-\rho t} dt$$

subject to

$$\dot{k}(t) = Ak(t) - c(t), \qquad k(0) = k_0, \quad \text{and} \quad k(t) \geq 0.$$

We can find an explicit solution for the social planner's problem. We use the dynamic programming approach, and write the Hamilton–Jacobi–Bellman equation:

$$\rho V(k) = \max_c [\ln c + V'(k)(Ak - c)], \qquad (19)$$

where $V(\cdot)$ is the value function, to be determined as part of the solution of the problem.

The first-order condition is

$$\frac{1}{c} = V'(k). \tag{20}$$

In addition, to ensure sufficiency, we impose the transversality condition[8]:

$$\lim_{t \to \infty} V(k(t))e^{-\rho t} = 0. \tag{21}$$

Substituting Equation (20) into Equation (19), we get

$$\rho V(k) = \ln 1 - \ln V'(k) + AkV'(k) - 1, \tag{22}$$

which is a first-order differential equation. We try a solution of the form[9]

$$V(k) = D + B \ln k.$$

Then $V'(k) = B/k$, and

$$\rho D + \rho B \ln k = -\ln B + \ln k + AB - 1.$$

For this equation to hold as an identity (i.e., for *all* $k > 0$), it must be the case that

$$\rho B \ln k = \ln k,$$

and

$$\rho D = -\ln B + AB - 1.$$

Thus,

$$B = \frac{1}{\rho},$$

and

$$D = \frac{1}{\rho}[\ln \rho + (A/\rho) - 1].$$

---

[8] See Dockner et al. (2000), particularly Chapter 3.
[9] For the properties of solution of a more general class of problem, see Long and Shimomura (1998).

It follows that the optimal solution for the social planner problem consists of the linear consumption strategy

$$c = \rho k = \frac{\rho}{A} y. \tag{23}$$

Thus, the optimal average propensity to consume is ρ/A. The rate of growth of the capital stock can be computed from

$$\dot{k} = Ak - c = Ak - \rho k,$$

implying that the endogenous growth rate is

$$g = \dot{k}/k = A - \rho > 0. \tag{24}$$

It follows that

$$k(t) = k_0 e^{(A-\rho)t}.$$

The value of the program is[10]

$$V(k_0) = \frac{1}{\rho}[\ln \rho + (A/\rho) - 1] + \frac{1}{\rho} \ln k_0. \tag{25}$$

4.1.2. The Laissez-Faire Outcome

Individuals take as given the time path of the economy's per capita wealth k. Individual i seeks to

$$\max_{c_i(t)} \int_0^\infty [\ln(c_i(t)) + \theta \ln(k_i(t)/k(t))] e^{-\rho t} dt \equiv V_i(k_{i0})$$

subject to

$$\dot{k_i} = Ak_i - c_i, \quad k_i(0) = k_{i0}, \quad \text{and} \quad k_i(t) \geq 0. \tag{26}$$

The Hamiltonian is

$$H_i = \ln(c_i(t)) + \theta \ln(k_i(t)/k(t)) + \psi_i(t)[Ak_i(t) - c_i(t)].$$

The necessary conditions are

$$\frac{\partial H_i}{\partial c_i} = \frac{1}{c_i} - \psi_i = 0 \tag{27}$$

$$\dot{\psi_i} = \rho \psi_i - \frac{\partial H_i}{\partial k_i} = (\rho - A)\psi_i - \frac{\theta}{k_i}. \tag{28}$$

---

[10] It can be verified that the transversality condition (21) is satisfied.

Differentiating Equation (27) with respect to t, we get

$$\frac{\dot{c}_i}{c_i} = -\frac{\dot{\psi}_i}{\psi_i}. \tag{29}$$

On the other hand, using Equation (28),

$$\frac{\dot{\psi}_i}{\psi_i} = \rho - A - \frac{\theta}{\psi_i k_i} = \rho - A - \frac{\theta c_i}{k_i}. \tag{30}$$

From Equations (29) and (30), we get

$$\frac{\dot{c}_i}{c_i} = \rho - A - \frac{\theta c_i}{k_i}. \tag{31}$$

To find a solution for the pair of differential equations (26) and (31), we guess that c_i is a linear function of k_i:

$$c_i = E_i k_i, \tag{32}$$

where E_i is to be determined. If Equation (32) holds, then

$$\frac{\dot{k}_i}{k_i} = \frac{\dot{c}_i}{c_i}.$$

Substituting Equation (32) into Equations (26) and (31), we obtain

$$A - E_i = \frac{\dot{k}_i}{k_i} = \frac{\dot{c}_i}{c_i} = \rho - A - \theta E_i.$$

This implies that

$$E_i = \frac{\rho}{1 + \theta}.$$

It follows that

$$c_i = \left[\frac{\rho}{1 + \theta}\right] \frac{y_i}{A} < \frac{\rho}{A} y_i. \tag{33}$$

The endogenous growth rate under laissez-faire is

$$\frac{\dot{k}_i}{k_i} = A - \frac{\rho}{1 + \theta} > A - \rho.$$

Proposition 2.3: Assume that individuals are wealth conscious ($\theta > 0$). Under laissez-faire, individuals consume a smaller fraction of their income than the fraction that the social planner would choose. This results in a higher growth rate under laissez-faire than under the social optimum. The greater is θ, the higher is the long-run growth rate. However, individuals are worse off under laissez-faire.

Remark 2.2: To verify that individuals are worse off under laissez-faire, let us calculate the integral of discounted utility under laissez-faire. Since $k_i/k = 1$ in equilibrium,

$$
\begin{aligned}
V_i(k_{i0}) &= \int_0^\infty [\ln c_i(t) + \theta \ln(1)]e^{-\rho t}\,dt \\
&= \int_0^\infty \left[\ln\left(\frac{\rho k_{i0}}{1+\theta} \exp(A - \rho/(1+\theta))t \right) \right] e^{-\rho t}\,dt \\
&= \frac{1}{\rho}[\ln\rho - \ln(1+\theta) + \ln k_{i0}] + (A - \rho/(1+\theta)) \int_0^\infty t e^{-\rho t}\,dt \\
&= \frac{1}{\rho}[\ln\rho - \ln(1+\theta) + \ln k_{i0}] + \frac{1}{\rho^2}\left[A - \frac{\rho}{1+\theta} \right]. \qquad (34)
\end{aligned}
$$

The difference between Equation (25) and Equation (34) is

$$
V(k_0) - V_i(k_{i0}) = \frac{1}{\rho}\left[\frac{A}{\rho} - 1 \right] - \frac{1}{\rho}\left[\frac{A}{\rho} - \frac{1}{1+\theta} - \ln(1+\theta) \right] > 0.
$$

(To see that the difference is positive, it is sufficient to show that $1 < (1/(1+\theta)) + \ln(1+\theta)$ for all $\theta > 0$. This is true because $(1/(1+\theta)) + \ln(1+\theta)$ is an increasing function of θ for all $\theta > 0$).

Remark 2.3: If we assume that the utility function is

$$
U(c_i, k_i, k) = \frac{1}{\beta}c_i^\beta + \frac{\theta}{\beta}\left[k_i^\beta - k^\beta \right]
$$

then the basic results of this section remain unchanged.

4.2. Case 2

4.2.1. The Social Planner's Problem

The social planner sets $k_i = k$ for all i. The objective is to maximize

$$
\max_{c(t)} \int_0^\infty \left[\left(\frac{c^\alpha}{\alpha} \right)(1+\theta) \right] e^{-\rho t}\,dt
$$

subject to $k = Ak - c$, $k(0) = k_0$, and $k(t) \geq 0$. The Hamiltonian is

$$H = \left(\frac{c^\alpha}{\alpha}\right)(1 + \theta) + \psi[Ak - c].$$

The necessary conditions are

$$(1 + \theta)c^{\alpha - 1} = \psi \tag{35}$$
$$\dot{\psi} = \psi(\rho - A). \tag{36}$$

Differentiate Equation (35) with respect to t to get

$$(\alpha - 1)\frac{\dot{c}}{c} = \frac{\dot{\psi}}{\psi} = \rho - A$$

or

$$\frac{\dot{c}}{c} = \frac{A - \rho}{1 - \alpha} = g > 0.$$

We also have, along a steady growth path,

$$\frac{\dot{k}}{k} = A - \frac{c}{k} = g.$$

Hence, under the assumption that

$$\rho - A\alpha > 0, \tag{37}$$

it is clear that the consumption/capital ratio is a positive constant:

$$\frac{c}{k} = A - g = \frac{A(1 - \alpha) - A + \rho}{1 - \alpha} = \frac{\rho - A\alpha}{1 - \alpha} > 0. \tag{38}$$

The transversality condition is satisfied:

$$\lim_{t \to \infty} e^{-\rho t}\psi(t)k(t) = \lim_{t \to \infty} e^{-\rho t}\psi(0)e^{(\rho - A)t}k(0)e^{gt}$$
$$= \lim_{t \to \infty} \psi(0)k(0)e^{-(A-g)t} = 0.$$

The optimal initial consumption is, from Equation (38),

$$c^*(0) = (A - g)k_0 > 0,$$

and

$$c^*(t) = c^*(0)e^{gt} = (A - g)k_0 e^{gt}.$$

The integral of discounted utility is

$$\int_0^\infty \left(\frac{1+\theta}{\alpha}\right)[(A-g)k_0e^{gt}]^\alpha e^{-\rho t}dt$$

$$= \left(\frac{1+\theta}{\alpha}\right)[(A-g)k_0]^\alpha \int_0^\infty e^{-(\rho-g\alpha)t}.$$

This integral converges because of Assumption (37).

4.2.2. The Laissez-Faire Outcome

It is easy to verify that, under laissez-faire, the outcome is a faster growth rate, but a lower level of well-being for all participants. The details are omitted for brevity.

5. CATCHING UP WHEN HOUSEHOLDS HAVE UNEQUAL INITIAL WEALTHS

5.1. The Model

We now return to the Cass–Ramsey model of Section 3, with a continuum of individuals, and add a complicating assumption: individuals have unequal initial stocks. The measure of the set of all individuals is normalized to unity. There are two groups of individuals: those who are initially poor and those who are initially wealthy. Their measures are α_1 and α_2, respectively, where $\alpha_1 + \alpha_2 = 1$. The initial capital stock of a poor individual is $k_1(0)$ and that of a wealthy one is $k_2(0) > k_1(0)$. Individuals earn the same wage rate, independently of their capital ownership. They take the time path of the overall capital–labor ratio, $k(t)$, as given. The question that interests us is whether the poor will catch up with the wealthy in the long run.

An early answer to this question was given by Stiglitz (1969), who assumed that individuals *do not* maximize utility over time. Stiglitz postulated that all individuals save a constant fraction s of their income. He demonstrated that in the long run all individuals will end up with the same amount of capital. Kemp and Shimomura (1992) considered the case where each individual maximizes the discounted value of the stream of his utility of consumption. They showed that inequality persists in the long run.

In this section, we reformulate the Kemp–Shimomura model by adding another variable in the utility function: relative wealth. We will show that if the elasticity of marginal utility of relative wealth is sufficiently high, individuals will end up with equal wealths.

The utility function of individual h (where $h = 1$ or $h = 2$) is

$$U_h\left(c_h, \frac{k_h}{k}\right) = u(c_h) + \theta v(z_h), \quad z_h \equiv \frac{k_h}{k},$$

where $k = \alpha_1 k_1 + \alpha_2 k_2$ and $\theta > 0$. Individuals have identical preferences: they have the same functions $u(\cdot)$ and $v(\cdot)$ and the same discount rate ρ. In what follows we set $\theta = 1$ without loss of generality. To simplify notation, we assume $\delta = 0$.

We assume that $v(z_h)$ is increasing and strictly concave in z_h. The strict convavity of $v(\cdot)$ means that $v'(z_h)$ is a decreasing function. This implies that a poor person gets more pleasure from a marginal increase in his relative wealth than a rich person. This provides a strong incentive for the poor to accumulate. Given the initial stock $k_h(0)$, individual h solves

$$\max \int_0^\infty \left[u(c_h(t)) + v\left(\frac{k_h(t)}{k(t)}\right)\right] e^{-\rho t} dt$$

subject to

$$\dot{k}_h(t) = r(t)k_h(t) + W(t) - c_h(t),$$

and

$$\lim_{t \to \infty} k_h(t) \exp\left[-\int_0^t r(\tau) d\tau\right] = 0.$$

To simplify notation, we will write v'_h for $v'(z_h)$ and u'_h for $u'(c_h)$ when there is no risk of confusion. Let σ_h denote the elaticity of marginal utility of consumption, and β_h the intertemporal rate of substitution:

$$\beta_h = \frac{1}{\sigma_h} = -\frac{u'_h}{c_h u''_h} > 0.$$

The Euler equation for the rich is

$$\frac{1}{\beta_1} \frac{\dot{c}_1}{c_1} = f'(k) - \rho + \left[\frac{v'_1}{k u'_1}\right] \tag{39}$$

and that for the poor is

$$\frac{1}{\beta_2}\frac{\dot{c}_2}{c_2} = f'(k) - \rho + \left[\frac{v_2'}{ku_2'}\right]. \tag{40}$$

The rates of change of their stocks of capital are

$$\dot{k}_1 = rk_1(t) - c_1 + W = f'(k)k_1 - c_1(t) + [f(k) - kf'(k)], \tag{41}$$

and

$$\dot{k}_2 = f'(k)k_2 - c_2 + [f(k) - kf'(k)]. \tag{42}$$

5.2. Steady States

Consider now the steady state of the system (39)–(42). Let the superscript * denote steady-state values. Then, setting the left-hand sides of Equations (41) and (42) to zero, we have

$$c_1^* - f'(k^*)k_1^* = c_2^* - f'(k^*)k_2^*. \tag{43}$$

Divide both sides by k_1^*:

$$\frac{c_1^*}{k_1^*} - f'(k^*) = \frac{c_2^*}{k_2^*}\frac{k_2^*}{k_1^*} - f'(k^*)\frac{k_2^*}{k_1^*}. \tag{44}$$

Next, setting the left-hand sides of Equations (39) and (40) to zero, we have

$$\frac{v'(z_1^*)}{u'(c_1^*)} = \frac{v'(z_2^*)}{u'(c_2^*)}. \tag{45}$$

It is easy to see that, for all α_i in $(0, 1)$ and $\alpha_j = 1 - \alpha_i$, there is always a "symmetric" steady state with $k_1^* = k_2^* = k^*$ and $c_1^* = c_2^* = f(k^*)$, with the property that

$$f'(k^*) - \rho + \frac{v'(1)}{k^*u'(f(k^*))} = 0, \tag{46}$$

provided that the function

$$\phi(k) \equiv f'(k) - \rho + \frac{v'(1)}{ku'(f(k))}$$

has the properties that $\phi(0) > 0$ and $\phi(\infty) < 0$. These properties are satisfied under the following assumptions.

Assumption A1:

(i) $f'(0) > \rho > f'(\infty)$

(ii) $\lim_{k \to \infty} u'(f(k))k = \infty$

For example, if $f(k) = k^\gamma$ and $u'(c) = c^{-\sigma}$, then Assumption A1 is satisfied if $\sigma\gamma < 1$.

Note, however, that Equation (46) may give several values for k^*. To ensure uniqueness of symmetric steady state, k^*, we make the following assumption.

Assumption A2: The capital share in national income is smaller than the elasticity of intertemporal substitution evaluated at steady-state consumption level:

$$\gamma(k) \equiv \frac{kf'(k)}{f(k)} < \beta(f(k)).$$

Proposition 2.4: Under Assumptions A1 and A2, we have existence and uniqueness of symmetric steady state. (The proof is left to the reader.)

In general, for any given steady-state aggregate capital stock k^*, one cannot exclude "asymmetric" steady state with $k_i^* \neq k_j^*$.

We now seek sufficient conditions that rule out asymmetric steady states. Note that any steady state (c_1, c_2, k_1, k_2) is a solution to the following system of equations:

$$c_1 = f'(k)k_1 + [f(k) - kf'(k)] \tag{47}$$

$$c_2 = f'(k)k_2 + [f(k) - kf'(k)] \tag{48}$$

$$0 = f'(k) - \rho + \frac{v'(k_1/k)}{ku'(c_1)} \tag{49}$$

$$0 = f'(k) - \rho + \frac{v'(k_2/k)}{ku'(c_2)}, \tag{50}$$

where $k = \alpha_1 k_1 + \alpha_2 k_2$. Suppose there is an asymmetric steady state, $(c_1^*, c_2^*, k_1^*, k_2^*)$, where $k_1^* \neq k_2^*$ and $c_1^* \neq c_2^*$. Then, for a given value $k^* = \alpha_1 k_1^* + \alpha_2 k_2^*$, consider, in the (k_h, c_h) space, the straight line

$$c_h = f'(k^*)k_h + [f(k^*) - k^* f'(k^*)] \tag{51}$$

with slope $dc_h/dk_h = f'(k^*)$, and the curve

$$0 = f'(k^*) - \rho + \frac{v'(k_h/k^*)}{k^* u'(c_h)}. \tag{52}$$

If there is an asymmetric steady state, then these two graphs must cut each other twice (at least); one of these points is (k_1^*, c_1^*) and the other is (k_2^*, c_2^*). Now the slope of Equation (51) is $f'(k^*)$, and the slope of Equation (52) is

$$\frac{dc_h}{dk_h} = \frac{u'v''}{k^* v'u''} = \beta(c_h)\eta(z_h)\frac{c_h}{k_h}, \tag{53}$$

where $\beta(c_h)$ is the inverse of the elasticity of marginal utility of consumption,

$$\beta(c_h) \equiv -\frac{u'(c_h)}{c_h u''(c_h)} > 0,$$

and $\eta(z_h)$ is the elasticity of marginal utility of relative wealth,

$$\eta(c_h) = -\frac{z_h v''(z_h)}{v'(z_h)} \geq 0.$$

Now if curve (52) cuts line (51) twice, then at one of these points, say point A, curve (52) cuts line (51) from above. At point A, the slope of curve (52) is smaller than the slope of the ray OA that goes through the origin O. It follows that, at A,

$$\frac{k_h}{c_h}\frac{dc_h}{dk_h} < 1. \tag{54}$$

In view of Equation (53), Condition (54) cannot be met if

$$\beta(c_h)\eta(z_h) \geq 1. \tag{55}$$

This consideration leads us to make the following assumption.

Assumption A3: For all nonnegative c_h, z_h, and k, the elasticity of marginal utility of relative wealth is at least as great as the elasticity of marginal utility of consumption; that is,

$$\eta(z_h) \geq \sigma(c_h). \tag{56}$$

We can now state our proposition on steady-state wealth distribution.

Proposition 2.5: Under Assumptions A1, A2, and A3, all individuals have identical steady-state wealth and consumption levels (i.e., asymmetric steady states do not exist).

Example: If

$$v(z_h) = \frac{z_h^{1-\sigma}}{1-\sigma} \quad \text{and} \quad u(c_h) = \frac{c_h^{1-\sigma}}{1-\sigma} \quad \text{for } h = i, j \tag{57}$$

then $\beta(c_h)\eta(z_h) = 1$, implying the nonexistence of asymmetric steady states. The steady-state aggregate capital stock, denoted by k^*, is determined by the following equation:

$$f'(k^*) - \rho = -\frac{v'(1)}{k^* u'(f(k^*))} = -\frac{(f(k^*))^\sigma}{k^*}.$$

5.3. Catching Up: Stability Analysis

We now examine the stability properties of symmetric steady states (without assuming that $\alpha_i = \alpha_j$). We must examine the local stability of system (39)–(42). Rewrite the system as follows:

$$k_1 = [f'(k)]k_1 - c_1 + [f(k) - kf'(k)] \tag{58}$$

$$k_2 = [f'(k)]k_2 - c_2 + [f(k) - kf'(k)] \tag{59}$$

$$\dot{c}_1 = \beta c_1 \left[f'(k) - \rho + \frac{v_1'}{ku_1'} \right] \tag{60}$$

$$\dot{c}_2 = \beta c_2 \left[f'(k) - \rho + \frac{v_2'}{ku_2'} \right]. \tag{61}$$

We linearize the system and then *evaluate all derivatives at the steady state*. We have the following matrix:

$$J \equiv \begin{bmatrix} a_{11} & a_{12} & -1 & 0 \\ a_{21} & a_{22} & 0 & -1 \\ a_{31} & a_{32} & a_{33} & 0 \\ a_{41} & a_{42} & 0 & a_{44} \end{bmatrix},$$

where

$$a_{11} = f' - (k^* - k_1^*)\alpha_1 f'' \quad (= f' \text{ at } k_1^* = k_2^* = k^*)$$

$$a_{12} = -\alpha_2(k^* - k_1^*) f'' \quad (= 0 \text{ at } k_1^* = k_2^* = k^*)$$

$$a_{21} = -\alpha_1(k^* - k_2^*) f'' \quad (= 0 \text{ at } k_1^* = k_2^* = k^*)$$

$$a_{22} = f' - (k^* - k_2^*)\alpha_2 f'' \quad (= f' \text{ at } k_1^* = k_2^* = k^*)$$

$$a_{31} = \beta\alpha_1 c_1^* \left[f'' - \frac{(1-\eta_1)v_1'}{k^2 u_1'} \right] + \frac{\beta c_1^* v_1''}{k^2 u_1'}, \quad \text{with } \eta_i \equiv -\frac{z_i^* v_i''}{v_i'} = -\frac{v''(1)}{v'(1)}$$

$$a_{32} = \beta\alpha_2 c_1^* \left[f'' - \frac{(1-\eta_1)v_1'}{k^2 u_1'} \right]$$

$$a_{32} = \rho - f' = -\frac{v_1'}{k u_1'} < 0$$

$$a_{41} = \beta\alpha_1 c_2^* \left[f'' - \frac{(1-\eta_2)v_2'}{k^2 u_2} \right]$$

$$a_{42} = \beta\alpha_2 c_2^* \left[f'' - \frac{(1-\eta_2)\theta v_2'}{k^2 u_2} \right] + \frac{\beta c_2^* v_2''}{k^2 u_2'}$$

$$a_{44} = \rho - f' = -\frac{v_2'}{k u_2'} < 0.$$

The following proposition can be proved.

Proposition 2.6: Under Assumptions A1, A2, and A3, the poor will be able to catch up with the rich.

Proof: See the Appendix. ∎

6. CONCLUDING REMARKS

We have shown that if relative wealth appears in the reduced-form utility function, then a number of standard results in the literature must be modified. In particular, under suitable curvature conditions, the poor will catch up with the rich in the long run. To fix ideas, we have referred to economic agents as individuals operating in a closed economy, but clearly they can be interpreted as nations in a globalized economy with perfectly mobile capital, so that factor prices are the same in all countries. Then our results say that poor nations will catch up with rich nations if the elasticity of marginal utility of relative wealth is sufficiently great.

In the context of an AK endogenous growth model, we showed that higher permanent growth rates will be achieved if individuals (or nations) are conscious about their relative wealth status. Such high growth rates, however, reduce welfare.

APPENDIX: PROOF OF PROPOSITION 2.6

We must examine the local stability of system (39)–(42). The characteristic equation is obtained by calculating the determinant of the matrix $xI - J$ and equating it to zero, where x is a scalar and I is the 4×4 identity matrix. Since $k_i^* = k_j^*$, we have $a_{12} = a_{21} = 0$. Substracting the third row of $xI - J$ by the first row times $[x - a_{33}]$, and substracting the fourth row by the second row times $[x - a_{44}]$, we obtain

$$
\det[xI - J] = \det \begin{bmatrix} x - f' & 0 & 1 & 0 \\ 0 & x - f' & 0 & 1 \\ -a_{31} - Y & -a_{32} & 0 & 0 \\ -a_{41} & -a_{42} - Y & 0 & 0 \end{bmatrix},
$$

where

$$
Y = (x - f')(x + f' - \rho) = (x - f')\left(x - \frac{v'}{ku'}\right). \tag{A1}
$$

Therefore,

$$
\begin{aligned}
\det[xI - J] &= (a_{31} + Y)(a_{42} + Y) - a_{41}a_{32} \\
&= Y^2 + (a_{31} + a_{42})Y + a_{31}a_{42} - a_{41}a_{32}.
\end{aligned}
$$

Let

$$
A \equiv f'' - \frac{(1 - \eta)v'(z^*)}{k^2 u'(c^*)}
$$

$$
B \equiv \frac{v''(z^*)}{k^2 u'(c^*)}.
$$

Then

$$a_{41}a_{31} = \alpha_1 \alpha_2 (\beta c^*)^2 A^2 > 0$$

$$a_{31}a_{42} = (\beta c^*)^2 (\alpha_1 A + B)(\alpha_2 A + B)$$
$$= a_{41}a_{31} + (\beta c^*)^2 \{B^2 + (\alpha_1 + \alpha_2) AB\}.$$

Thus,

$$a_{31}a_{42} - a_{41}a_{32} = (\beta c^*)^2 B(B + A) \equiv d.$$

Note that

$$d \equiv a_{31}a_{42} - a_{41}a_{32} > 0$$
$$\text{if} \quad G \equiv f'' - \frac{(1 - \eta)v'(z^*)}{k^2 u'(c^*)} + \frac{v''(z^*)}{k^2 u'(c^*)} < 0. \qquad (A2)$$

Lemma A1: At the steady state, d is positive.

Proof: Using the fact that $z^* = 1$ at a symmetric steady state, write G as

$$G = f'' - \frac{(1 - \eta)v'}{k^2 u'} - \frac{\eta v'}{k^2 u'} = f'' - \frac{v'}{k^2 u'} < 0.$$

Next,

$$a_{31} + a_{42} = \beta c^* [\alpha_j A + B] + \beta c^* [\alpha_i A + B] = \beta c^* (A + 2B) \equiv b.$$

Thus, the characteristic equation is

$$\det[xI - J] = d + bY + Y^2 = 0, \qquad (A3)$$

which is a quadratic in Y. The two roots are

$$Y_{1,2} = \frac{-b \pm \sqrt{\Delta}}{2},$$

where

$$\Delta = b^2 - 4d = (\beta c^*)^2 [A^2 + 4B^2 + 4AB - 4B(B + A)]$$
$$= (\beta c^*)^2 A^2.$$

Thus,

$$Y_1 = -B\beta c^* > 0 \quad \text{if} \quad v'' < 0,$$

and

$$Y_2 = -[B + A]\beta c^* = -\beta c^* \left[f'' - \frac{(1-\eta)\theta v'(z^*)}{k^2 u'(c^*)} + \frac{v''(z^*)}{k^2 u'(c^*)} \right].$$

Substituting Y_1 into Equation (A1), we get

$$(x - f')\left(x - \frac{v'}{ku'}\right) - Y_1 = x^2 - x\left(f' + \frac{v'}{ku'}\right) + \frac{\theta v' f'}{ku'}$$
$$+ \frac{\beta c^* v''(z^*)}{k^2 u'(c^*)} = 0,$$

hence,

$$x^2 - \left(f' + \frac{\theta v'}{ku'}\right)x + \frac{\theta v'}{k^2 u'}\left[k^* f' + \beta c^* \frac{v''(z^*)}{v'(z^*)}\right] = 0. \qquad (A4)$$

Now since $z^* = 1$

$$-\frac{v''(z^*)}{v'(z^*)} \equiv \frac{\eta}{z^*} = \eta.$$

Assume Equation (56) holds. Then $\eta\beta \geq 1$, and

$$k^* f' - \beta\eta c^* \leq k^* f' - c^* = -[f(k^*) - k^* f'(k^*)] < 0.$$

(from Equation (58)), and equation (A4) has two real roots of opposite sign.

Similarly, substituting Y_2 into Equation (A1), we get

$$(x - f')\left(x - \frac{v'}{ku'}\right) - Y_1 = x^2 - x\left(f' + \frac{v'}{ku'}\right) + \frac{v' f'}{ku'}$$
$$+ \frac{\beta c^* v''}{k^2 u'} + \beta c^* \left[f'' - \frac{(1-\eta)v'}{k^2 u'}\right],$$

hence,

$$x^2 - \left(f' + \frac{v'}{ku'}\right)x + Q = 0, \qquad (A5)$$

where

$$Q \equiv \frac{v'}{k^2 u'}\left[k^* f' + \beta c^* \frac{v''}{v'}\right] + \beta c^* \left[f'' - \frac{(1-\eta)v'}{k^2 u'}\right]. \qquad \blacksquare$$

Lemma A2: Q is negative if

$$\beta \geq \gamma(k), \tag{A6}$$

where $\gamma(k)$ is the share of capital income in national income:

$$\gamma(k) \equiv \frac{kf'(k)}{f} > 0.$$

Proof:

$$Q = \beta c^* f'' + \frac{v'}{k^2 u'} \left[k^* f' + \beta c^* \left(\frac{v''}{v'} - (1 - \eta) \right) \right]$$

$$= \beta c^* f'' + \frac{v'}{k^2 u'} [k^* f' - \beta c^*],$$

where $c^* = f(k^*)$. Thus, $Q < 0$ if Inequality (A6) holds. ∎

Lemma A3: Equation (A5) has two real roots of opposite signs if Inequality (A6) holds.

Proposition 2.7: If

$$\beta \geq \max \left[\gamma(k), \frac{1}{\eta(z)} \right] \tag{A7}$$

then there are four real roots, two of which are negative, implying that the steady state is stable in the saddlepoint sense. This implies that the poor will be able to catch up with the rich.

REFERENCES

Akerlof, George A. (1976), "The Economics of the Caste and of the Rat Race and Other Woeful Tales," *Quarterly Journal of Economics* 90: 599–617.

Cole, Harold L., George J. Mailath, and Andrew Postlewaite (1992), "Social Norms, Savings Behavior, and Growth," *Journal of Political Economy* 100(6): 1092–1125.

Dawkins, Richard (1976), *The Selfish Gene*, Oxford University Press, Oxford, UK.

Dawkins, Richard (1986), *The Blind Watchmaker*, Oxford University Press, Oxford, UK.

Dockner, Engelbert, Steffan Jorgensen, Ngo Van Long, and Gerhard Sorger (2000), *Differential Games in Economics and Management Science*, Cambridge University Press, Cambridge, UK.

Kemp, Murray C., and Koji Shimomura (1992), "A Dymamic Model of the Distribution of Wealth among Households and Nations," *Annals of Operations Research* 37: 245–72.

Konrad, Kai A. (1992), "Wealth-Seeking Reconsidered," *Journal of Economic Behavior and Organization* 18(2): 215–27.

Long, Ngo Van, and Koji Shimomura (1998), "Some Results on the Markov Equilibria of a Class of Homogenous Differential Games," *Journal of Economic Behavior and Organization* 33: 557–66.

Long, Ngo Van, and Koji Shimomura (2003), "A New Proof of the Maximum Principle," *Economic Theory* 22: 671–74.

Long, Ngo Van, and Kar-yiu Wong (1997), "Endogenous Growth and International Trade: A Survey," in B. Jensen and Kar-yiu Wong (eds.), *Dynamics, Economic Growth, and International Trade*, University of Michigan Press, pp. 11–74. Ann Arbor, Michigan.

Pitchford, John D. (1960), "Growth and the Elasticity of Factor Substitution," *Economic Record* 36: 491–504.

Solow, Robert M. (1956), "A Contribution to the Theory of Economic Growth," *Quarterly Journal of Economics* 70: 65–94.

Stiglitz, J. E. (1969), "Distribution of Income and Wealth among Individuals," *Econometrica* 37(3): 382–97.

Van Valen, Leigh (1973), "A New Evolutionary Law," *Evolutionary Theory* 1: 1–30.

Wynne-Edwards, V. C. (1962), *Animal Dispersion in Relation to Social Behaviour*, Oliver and Boyd, Edinburgh.

3

Knowledge and Development:
A Schumpeterian Approach

Philippe Aghion, Cecilia García-Peñalosa, and Peter Howitt

1. INTRODUCTION

It is easy to get discouraged when pondering the economic situation of the world's poorest countries. The large-scale international development programs that have been under way for the past half century have fallen short of solving the problems of disease, malnutrition, illiteracy, and poverty that keep people in less developed countries (LDCs) from enjoying the prosperity we take for granted in the industrialized world. In terms of per capita real income, which is arguably the best single indicator of a country's level of economic development, the gap between rich and poor has been growing exponentially. For example, in 1960 the average per capita real income of the richest 10% of countries was more than 12 times that of the poorest 10%. Since then the average income of the richest 10% has tripled, while that of the poorest 10% has remained roughly constant.

Economics provides no magic formula for closing the development gap: that is why our discipline is known as the dismal science. However, in this chapter we shall argue that the task is not as impossible as it might *a priori* seem: reflecting on how technology has rescued people from economic difficulties in the past provides at least reason to believe that the prospects of low-income countries in the 21st century are somewhat brighter than one might otherwise think and to gain faith in the growth-enhancing effects of policies aimed at facilitating the creation and the diffusion of *technological knowledge*.

A main lesson from the history of the past two centuries is that salvation has often come in the form of new technological knowledge. A first example is the Green Revolution undertaken in the early postwar period to create and disseminate new agricultural technologies. As a result of this policy, the number of varieties of rice doubled between 1966 and 1985. More generally, even though the world's population exploded since Malthus wrote his celebrated "Essay on Population," the world's food supply has exploded even faster: we produce far more food per person each year now than was produced 200 years ago. Although famines still occasionally occur, the reason is not because the world has too little food but rather because those who can afford more than they need will not share enough with those who cannot. Malthus's prediction that most of humanity was doomed to live forever on the verge of starvation was based on the presupposition that population should eventually grow faster than food supply as more and more people would be working with limited (land) resources. However, this reasoning failed to anticipate technological progress. Whereas no one repealed the law of diminishing returns or abolished scarcity, we have learned how to produce more food from any given combination of inputs of land, labor, and capital; we have learned better techniques of animal husbandry, fertilization, irrigation, crop rotation, and disease control; we have learned to produce better farm implements, better varieties of seeds, and so on. In short, the world has experienced enormous technological progress in food production, which in turn has offset the otherwise disastrous consequences of diminishing returns.

A second example is the oil crisis of the early 1970s: the fear developed in industrialized countries that the world was heading for disaster as a result of using up its natural resources, in particular the supply of fossil fuels. In the 1970s, while the industrialized world was experiencing a drastic run-up in oil prices, well-respected economists were predicting that the price of oil would continue to rise exponentially, in inflation-adjusted terms, to the point where by the start of the 21st century it would be three times the level of the mid-1970s. What actually happened was again a case of technological progress. Human ingenuity was spurred by the rise in the price of energy in the 1970s, and as a result we have learned to produce motor vehicles and home-heating systems that are vastly more fuel efficient than anything imaginable at that time. Not only have we discovered new oil reserves (e.g, in the North Sea), but we have also made tremendous strides in reducing the cost of extracting oil from the sea and from the Athabaska tar sands, Thus, again, *the problem of diminishing returns has been alleviated by the creation and diffusion of knowledge that can be used to satisfy our needs more efficiently, so that we are less constrained than we used to be by the finiteness of our basic resources.*

In this chapter, we take "knowledge" to reflect the ability of individuals or groups of individuals to undertake, or instruct or induce others to undertake, procedures resulting in predictable transformations of material objects. Knowledge so defined can be codifiable, as when it can be transmitted by mathematical theorems or computer programs that can be reproduced through known procedures, or it can be tacit, as when it exists only in the mind of particular individuals or in the established routines of organizations, and is not capable of routine transmission or reproduction.

There are many ways in which a piece of knowledge thus defined is like a capital good. It can be produced, exchanged, and used in the production of other goods or in its own (re)production. It can also be stored, although subject to depreciation, as when people forget or let their skills deteriorate; it is also subject to obsolescence, as when new knowledge comes along to supersede it. Yet our main purpose in this chapter is to argue that growth theories that treat knowledge purely as a capital good are bound to miss important aspects of the growth process both in high- and low-income countries; in contrast, the Schumpeterian growth paradigm, where knowledge creation and diffusion result primarily from innovative activities and investments, has the potential to deliver more reliable predictions and also more detailed policy prescriptions on the determinants of economic development.

In the first part of the chapter, Creating Knowledge, we show how the Schumpeterian framework, unlike the neoclassical or AK models based on capital accumulation, can provide insights on the impact of institutions, legislations, and policy on the rate of knowledge creation and thereby on the rate of productivity growth. We also show that in both the neoclassical and the AK paradigms long-run growth is unsustainable in an economy with limited input resources; in contrast, if we take a Schumpeterian approach to knowledge creation and growth, government policy can sustain a positive rate of growth in output or consumer utility by inducing the right kind and/or rate of resource-saving innovations.

In the second part of the chapter, Absorbing Knowledge, we turn our attention to cross-country knowledge spillovers and to the process of cross-country convergence. What reasons do we have to think that technology can work the same wonders for the poor as it has for the rich? One reason certainly lies in the late-20th-century experience of East Asian countries such as Hong Kong, Taiwan, Singapore, South Korea, and China. In 1960 their per capita real incomes were far below that of the United States, but since then they have grown on average at more than 5% per year, even taking into account the setbacks that some of them experienced in the financial crisis that began in 1998. Several of these countries now have per capita real incomes that are close to those of members of the Organisation for Economic Co-operation and Development, and they seem likely to catch up with the United States in another few decades. On the other hand, many among the poorer African countries have barely grown at all during the past three decades and seem to be stuck in a low-development trap. What are the main factors that account for this dual – or " club" – convergence path?

In the second part of the chapter, we shall emphasize research and development (R&D) investments, education, and also several aspects of what we refer to as "openness" to new knowledge as key determinants of lower income countries' ability to learn from more technologically advanced countries and thereby to catch up with them. In particular, we shall argue that the Schumpeterian approach to global growth, based on the diffusion of technological knowledge from richer to poorer countries, provides a better account of the process of cross-country convergence than the neoclassical models in which convergence is entirely driven by diminishing returns to capital accumulation.

2. CREATING KNOWLEDGE

2.1. The Need for Growth Models Where Knowledge Creation Is Endogenous

The idea that knowledge creation is critical for long-run economic growth is certainly the most important proposition that emerges from the neoclassical theory of Solow (1956) and Swan (1956). More specifically, consider a closed economy in which final output Y is produced each period using the current capital stock K, according to the production technology

$$Y = F(K, AL),$$

where (i) A is a productivity parameter that measures the current state of knowledge; (ii) L is the current size of the labor force; and (iii) the production technology F exhibits diminishing returns to capital accumulation; that is, the marginal productivity of capital F_K decreases as capital accumulates.

Capital accumulates according to the accumulation equation

$$\frac{dK}{dt} = sY - \delta K, \tag{AC}$$

where s is the fraction of savings – assumed to be constant in the Solow–Swan model – and δ is the depreciation rate of capital.

In the absence of population growth (i.e., if L remains constant) and of technical progress (i.e., if A too remains constant), such an economy cannot grow forever at a positive rate. Indeed, because of diminishing returns to capital, national income Y does not grow as fast as the capital stock, which in turn means that savings sY cannot grow as fast as depreciation. Eventually depreciation catches up with savings and at that point the capital stock stops rising and the economy stops growing. With population growth, and a production technology F that exhibits constant returns with respect to K and L, the same reasoning can be applied to output per capita $y = Y/L$, which is then a concave function of capital per capita $k = K/L$. We then obtain the proposition that knowledge creation (i.e., a growing A) is necessary in order to sustain long-run growth of income per capita when final production exhibits decreasing returns to capital accumulation.

Whereas knowledge creation, which determines the long-run rate of growth of income per capita, is taken as given by neoclassical growth models from Solow (1956) to Mankiw et al. (1992), a main proposition shared by the so-called endogenous growth models is that knowledge is generated by the economic system itself. There are two variants of endogenous growth theory. The first variant, known as AK theory, was introduced in a long-neglected contribution by Frankel (1962) and then given its modern formulation in the celebrated articles of Romer (1986) and Lucas (1988). The AK model, which we analyze in the next subsection, treats knowledge as little more than a particular kind of capital: namely, knowledge creation results directly from capital accumulation by the different firms in the economy, where the basic idea is that capital accumulation by any individual firm contributes to a collective process of creation of new technological and organizational knowledge through learning by doing or learning by imitating. Such knowledge creation, in turn, will permanently offset the effect of the diminishing marginal productivity of capital and thereby enable the economy to sustain a positive rate of growth in the long run under suitable assumptions on the learning externalities.

The second variant of endogenous growth theory is the Schumpeterian approach,[1] which revolves around the following set of ideas:

(i) A main source of technological progress is innovation.

(ii) Innovations, which lead to the introduction of new production processes, new products, new management methods, and new organization of production activities, are created by self-interested firms, entrepreneurs, and researchers who expect to be rewarded with (monopoly) rents in the event that their innovation is successfully implemented.[2]

(iii) In general, these monopoly rents are eventually dissipated as the new processes or products introduced by current innovators become obsolete when new innovations occur that compete with the current technologies and, thereby, drive them out of the market; this is the Schumpeterian notion of "creative destruction."

Unlike its AK predecessors, the Schumpeterian model emphasizes the distinctness of R&D from other investments in physical or human capital. As we shall argue in the next subsection, by focusing on knowledge creation as a distinct source of productivity growth separated from capital accumulation, the Schumpeterian approach makes it possible first to provide a more detailed account of the economic and institutional determinants of (long-run) growth, and second to conceive of the possibility that growth be made sustainable in an economy with limited natural input resources. Furthermore, as we shall argue in the following section, the Schumpeterian approach can be reconciled with existing evidence on cross-country convergence in a way

---

[1] This approach, which builds on Aghion and Howitt's earlier work (1992), is developed at length by Aghion and Howitt (1998). See also Romer (1990) for an R&D-based model of growth that does not embody the Schumpeterian notion of creative destruction, and Grossman and Helpman (1991) for a quality-ladder model with unit elastic demands that combines Aghion and Howitt (1992) with Segerstrom et al. (1990).

[2] Of course, knowledge creation also depends on progress in basic science, which often is driven by curiosity rather than profit. Yet much of the research that has led to fundamental breakthroughs in basic science has been conducted by private for-profit business firms.

that outperforms the neoclassical approach developed by Mankiw et al. (1992).

2.2. The Limits of the AK Approach

First introduced by Frankel (1962) to reconcile the assumption of diminishing returns to individual capital accumulation with the possibility of positive long-run growth as in the Harrod–Domar model, the AK model features a competitive economy with N firms. Each firm $j\,(1 \leq j \leq N)$ produces final output according to the Cobb–Douglas production function:

$$Y_j = AK_j^{\alpha}L_j^{1-\alpha}, \tag{1}$$

where (i) α is strictly less than one, so that there are diminishing returns to individual capital accumulation; and (ii) A is a productivity parameter that reflects the current state of knowledge. While the dynamic evolution of A, (i.e., knowledge creation) is taken as given in the neoclassical model, the AK model endogenizes knowledge creation by making it the *collective* outcome of capital accumulation by all firms in the economy. More formally, it assumes

$$A = A_0 \left(\frac{1}{N}\sum_j K_j\right)^{\eta}, \tag{2}$$

where η measures the degree of externality in firms' learning by doing.

For simplicity let $L_j \equiv 1$ for all j; then, in a symmetric equilibrium where $K_j = K/N$ for all j, aggregate per capita income Y will satisfy the following equation:

$$Y = A_0 N^{1-\alpha-\eta} K^{\alpha+\eta}. \tag{3}$$

This, together with the accumulation equation (AC), which still holds here if we assume a constant savings rate, will determine the entire growth path of the economy. We shall be particularly interested in the knife-edge case where $\alpha + \eta = 1$. Only then will the long-run rate of growth g be finitely positive, equal to

$$g = sA_0 - \delta, \tag{4}$$

which is nothing but the Harrod–Domar growth rate.

A major criticism to this approach, most forcefully put forward by Mankiw et al. (1992), is that, unless $\alpha + \eta < 1$ (in which case, as in the neoclassical model where $\eta = 0$, the long-run rate of growth in output per capita is equal to zero), this model cannot account for conditional convergence, which is convergence among countries with similar production characteristics (i.e., with the same values of the parameters A_0, α, δ, and η). As we shall now argue, another drawback of the AK approach is that it cannot account for the possibility of sustained positive optimal growth in an economy in which capital accumulation requires the use of an exhaustible resource. That the issue of sustainable development might be more adequately analyzed using an optimal growth formulation a la Cass–Koopmans has been convincingly argued by Dasgupta (1994), who defines "sustainable development" as development that maximizes the total (discounted) welfare of current *and* future generations, taking into account not only the constraints imposed by the finiteness of natural resources but also all the possibilities for technological substitution between different kinds of capital goods, be they physical, natural, or intellectual.

We shall thus abandon the constant savings rate assumption and replace it by intertemporal utility maximization by a representative infinitely lived consumer who incarnates a representative dynasty over time. The following variant of the AK model will thus be very similar to that of Romer (1986) except for the introduction of a limited natural resource that must be depleted in order to produce capital. As it turns out, this addition to the AK model will dramatically affect its ability to explain long-run growth.

More formally, consider the following AK model with limited natural resources. At each period, final output is produced using capital and a flow of natural resource services, R, according to the production technology

$$Y = AKR^v, \tag{5}$$

where $0 < v < 1$. The current stock of natural resources is denoted by S, and this stock depletes as resource services are being provided to the final sector, namely,

$$\dot{S} = -R. \tag{6}$$

The optimal growth path is then one that maximizes intertemporal utility of the representative consumer, that is, one which solves

$$\max W = \int_0^\infty e^{-\rho t} u(c_t) dt$$

subject to Equations (5) and (6) and the resource constraints

$$\dot{K} = Y - c \tag{7}$$

$$S \geq 0. \tag{8}$$

The Hamiltonian for this program is

$$H = u(c) + \lambda(AKR^\nu - c) - \xi R, \tag{9}$$

where λ and ξ are the shadow prices associated with constraints (6) and (7). Now, taking isoelastic utility functions of the form $u(c) = (c^{1-\varepsilon} - 1)/(1 - \varepsilon)$, the first-order conditions satisfied by the optimal solution to this program are

$$\dot{\lambda} - \rho\lambda = -\frac{\partial H}{\partial K}, \tag{10}$$

$$0 = \frac{\partial H}{\partial c}, \tag{11}$$

and

$$\dot{\xi} - \rho\xi = -\frac{\partial H}{\partial S} = 0.$$

The first two conditions together lead to the well-known Ramsey equation:

$$\frac{\dot{c}}{c} = \frac{1}{\varepsilon}(AR^\nu - \rho), \tag{12}$$

The unnumbered equation implies that the shadow price of the natural resource, ξ, grows exponentially at rate ρ over time. Thus, ξ converges to infinity in the long run. Furthermore, Equations (6) and (8) immediately imply that R must eventually converge to zero. This, together with the Ramsey equation, Equation (12), rules out the possibility that optimal growth is positive in the long run because this would lead to the contradiction $\dot{c}/c \rightarrow -\rho/\varepsilon$.

In other words, unbounded growth cannot go on forever because the resource constraint will eventually reduce the marginal social value of capital below the discount rate ρ. And here, unlike in the AK model without limited resources, the accumulation of knowledge is of no help. Indeed, to the extent that new knowledge is entirely driven by capital accumulation in this model, a faster rate of technical progress would require speeding up the depletion of the natural resource, which in turn can only lower the prospects for sustained long-run growth, namely, aggravate the problem that technical progress was supposed to alleviate!

In contrast, the Schumpeterian model, which treats technological innovations and capital accumulation as two separate processes, will now be shown to accommodate the possibility of a positive optimal long-run rate of growth.

2.3. A Schumpeterian Model with Capital Accumulation

The Schumpeterian model spelled out in this subsection will be used repeatedly in the remaining part of this chapter. As we shall try to argue, compared to both the neoclassical and the AK models, this Schumpeterian framework should have the potential to deliver (i) a more detailed account of the economic factors underlying knowledge creation and long-run growth, (ii) a more optimistic perspective on sustainable development under limited resource constraints, (iii) a richer and also more convincing approach to cross-country convergence, and (iv) a more adequate framework to discuss policy issues related to the creation and diffusion of knowledge.

Consider the following extension of work by Aghion and Howitt (1992). There is one final good, which can be used both for consumption purposes and in the production of intermediate inputs. This final good is produced according to the production technology

$$Y = L^{1-\alpha} \int_0^1 A_i x_i^\alpha \, di, \qquad (13)$$

where L is the labor flow used in final good manufacturing, x_i is the quantity of input i currently used to produce final output, and A_i is a productivity parameter measuring the quality of the latest version of input i. (For simplicity, we omit the time subscript t in this equation.)

Intermediate inputs are all produced using capital according to the production function

$$x_i = \frac{K_i}{A_i}, \qquad (14)$$

where K_i is the input of capital in sector i. Division by A_i reflects the fact that successive vintages of intermediate input i are produced by increasingly capital-intensive techniques.

Knowledge creation, that is, technological innovations, are targeted at specific intermediate goods. An innovation in sector i will give rise to an improved version of intermediate good i, and at the same time it will allow the innovator to replace the incumbent monopolist until the next innovation occurs in that sector.[3] The incumbent monopolist in each intermediate sector i operates with a price schedule given by the marginal productivity of input i, namely,

$$p_i = A_i \alpha x_i^{\alpha-1} L^{1-\alpha},$$

and a linear cost function

$$C(x_i) = (r + \delta - \beta)K_i = (r + \delta - \beta)A_i x_i,$$

where r is the current interest rate (again, for notational simplicity we omit the time subscript t), δ is the fixed rate of depreciation, and β is the rate at which capital accumulation is subsidized. Thus, if for simplicity we normalize the aggregate supply of labor L to one, the incumbent monopolist in sector i will choose x_i to maximize

$$\max \left\{ A_i \alpha x_i^{\alpha-1} . x_i - (r + \delta - \beta)A_i x_i \right\} = \pi_i.$$

It is immediately seen that the solution x to this maximization program is independent of i; that is, in equilibrium all intermediate firms will supply the same quantity of intermediate product. This in turn implies that, for all i,

$$\frac{K_i}{A_i} \equiv x \equiv \frac{K}{A} \equiv k,$$

where $K = \int K_i di$ is the aggregate demand for capital, which in equilibrium is equal to the aggregate supply of capital; $A = \int A_i di$ is the average productivity parameter across all sectors; and, therefore, $k = K/A$ is the capital stock per effective worker. The first-order

---

[3] In this model, as in Aghion and Howitt's (1992), no innovations are done by incumbents; this, in turn, is a direct consequence (i) of new knowledge becoming immediately accessible to nonincumbent researchers; (ii) of the Arrow (or replacement) effect, namely, the incremental postinnovation profit of an incumbent firm is less than that of a nonincumbent firm since the incumbent firm already enjoys positive monopoly rents; and (iii) the research technology is linear.

condition for the preceding maximization program can then be simply rewritten as

$$\alpha^2 k^{\alpha-1} = r + \delta - \beta. \tag{K}$$

We shall refer to this first equilibrium condition as the *capital equation* and denote it by (K). The second condition will be an analogue of the Aghion–Howitt (AH) research-arbitrage equation (1992, 1998), which we now derive as follows.

As in AH (1992), innovations result from R&D investments, but here we suppose that, instead of using labor as a unique input, the R&D sectors use final output or, equivalently, they use labor and capital services according to the same Cobb–Douglas technology as in the final-good sector. An innovation in sector i at date t will bring this sector's productivity parameter A_i up to the current leading-edge productivity level, $A^{max} = \max_j A_j$, at that date. This implicitly assumes that the leading-edge technology, once discovered, is automatically disclosed and consequently becomes immediately accessible to all potential innovators. Thus, while the incumbent innovator in any sector has monopoly power over the use of his innovation, the knowledge embodied in this innovation is publicly accessible to all producers engaged in R&D activities aimed at generating further innovations.

Innovations in any intermediate sector are assumed to follow a Poisson process with arrival rate, λn, where λ is a parameter that measures the productivity of R&D and n is the productivity-adjusted quantity of final output devoted to R&D or, more precisely, the amount of R&D expenditure per intermediate good divided by the leading-edge productivity level A^{max}.[4] We divide by A^{max} to reflect the fact that, as technology advances, the resource cost of further advances increases proportionally.[5]

The research-arbitrage condition determining the equilibrium level of R&D simply says that the net marginal cost of R&D – namely, $1 - \psi$, where ψ is the rate at which R&D is subsidized (or taxed, if $\psi < 0$) – is equal to the expected productivity-adjusted value generated by *one* unit of final output being invested in R&D; this expected value is equal to λ / A^{max} times the value of an innovation in any intermediate good

---

[4] Obviously remains proportional to the average productivity in steady state.
[5] This "diminishing opportunities" hypothesis is discussed and analyzed in detail by Kortum (1997).

sector, which in turn is equal to

$$V = \frac{\pi}{r + \lambda n}, \tag{15}$$

where

$$\pi = \max_{x_i} \left\{ A_i \alpha x_i^{\alpha-1} \cdot x_i - (r + \delta - \beta) A_i x_i \right\}$$
$$= A^{\max} \cdot \tilde{\pi}(k) = A^{\max} \alpha (1 - \alpha) k^{\alpha}.$$

(Here we implicitly use the fact that the innovation pushes productivity A_i in sector i up to the *current* leading-edge level $A^{\max}$.) The denominator of Equation (15) is the discount rate on incumbent innovations; it is equal to the interest rate plus the rate of creative destruction λn, that is, the flow probability of being displaced by a new innovation occurring in the same sector. Hence, we obtain the following simple research-arbitrage equation, which we refer to as (R):

$$1 - \psi = \lambda \frac{\tilde{\pi}(k)}{r + \lambda n}. \tag{R}$$

Equations (K) and (R) together determine the equilibrium steady-state level of R&D as a function of the parameters of the economy. In particular, taking the interest rate as given,[6] equilibrium R&D will be encouraged either by an increase in the subsidy rate of R&D ψ or by an increase in the subsidy rate of capital β; it will also increase with the productivity of R&D λ. It will be discouraged by an increase in the cost of capital (e.g., following an increase in the depreciation rate δ). Finally, it will respond positively to patent legislations aimed at protecting innovators against the risk of imitation. (If innovations could be imitated at Poisson rate p, then the denominator on the right-hand side of (R) should be replaced by $r + \lambda n + p$.)

Now, to go from R&D to growth, we assume the existence of cross-sector knowledge spillovers which cause the leading-edge productivity $A^{\max}$ to grow at a rate proportional to the flow of innovations in the economy; that is,

$$\frac{\dot{A}^{\max}}{A^{\max}} = \lambda n \sigma = g, \tag{16}$$

where $\sigma > 0$ measures the size of cross-sector spillovers. Then, the preceding comparative statics on equilibrium R&D will immediately

---

[6] In equilibrium, assuming isoelastic preferences for the representative consumer, we also have the Ramsey equation: where is the rate of time preference.

carry over to the equilibrium growth rate g, which in steady state is also the growth rate of *average* productivity (i.e., $\dot{A}/A = g$, because the distribution of productivity ratios $A_i/A^{\max}$ is then stationary).

Having thus determined the equilibrium rate of knowledge creation and growth as a function of the basic parameters of the economy, we may now reconsider the issue of sustainable development using this Schumpeterian framework instead of the AK approach. Thus, suppose that final output is produced each period according to

$$Y = L^\eta R^\nu \int_0^1 A_i x_i^\alpha \, di, \tag{17}$$

where R again denotes the current flow of services from the natural resource, and $\alpha + \nu + \eta = 1$. In equilibrium, we know that all intermediate sectors will produce the same amount of intermediate goods $x = K/A$, so that we simply have

$$Y = A^{1-\alpha} K^\alpha L^\eta R^\nu. \tag{18}$$

The optimal growth path is one that maximizes intertemporal utility of the representative consumer subject to the same constraints as in the preceding sub-section, but with this modified expression for Y and also the spillover equation

$$\frac{\dot{A}^{\max}}{A^{\max}} = \frac{\dot{A}}{A} = \lambda n \sigma.$$

Again, let us normalize aggregate labor supply at $L = 1$. Then, assuming isoelastic preferences for the representative consumer, with $u(c) = (c^{1-\varepsilon} - 1)/(1 - \varepsilon)$, the Ramsey equation corresponding to this optimal growth problem can be written as follows:

$$\frac{\dot{c}}{c} = \frac{1}{\varepsilon}\left(\frac{\partial Y}{\partial K} - \rho - \delta\right) = \frac{1}{\varepsilon}\left(\alpha\left(\frac{A}{K}\right)^{1-\alpha} R^\nu - \rho - \delta\right). \tag{19}$$

Now, unlike in the preceding sub-section, the marginal social value of capital $(\alpha(A/K)^{1-\alpha} R^\nu - \delta)$ can remain constant and strictly positive over time even if we impose a finiteness constraint on natural resources. Indeed, whereas in the AK model, knowledge A was bound to grow at exactly the same rate as the supply of capital K so that $\partial Y/\partial K \approx R^\nu$ would eventually become less than ρ; here, by adequately adjusting the growth rate of R&D spending (i.e., by adjusting n), one can hope that knowledge A will grow sufficiently faster than K in order to offset the effect of a falling R on long-run growth. For example, suppose that the government aims at a depletion rate of the natural resource, equal to some positive q; that is,

$$\frac{\dot{R}}{R} = -q. \tag{20}$$

Then, in order to maintain the growth rate of consumption constant at some level g_0, it suffices to target the growth rate of R&D spending n at a level such that $(A/K)^{1-\alpha} R^v$ remains constant over time or, equivalently, using the fact that in steady state $\dot{A}/A = \lambda n\sigma$ and $\dot{K}/K = \dot{c}/c = g_0$ and taking logarithmic derivatives:

$$\frac{d\left(\ln\left((A/K)^{1-\alpha} R^v\right)\right)}{dt} = (1-\alpha)(\lambda n\sigma - g_0) - vq = 0. \tag{21}$$

In particular, when λ and σ are sufficiently large, there will always exist a feasible rate n^*, which is an equilibrium that can be achieved through a suitable policy choice (β, ψ) (i.e., of capital and R&D subsidies), which satisfies Equation (21).

Thus, whereas the stock of natural resources is bound to deplete, knowledge creation and adequately "green" innovations should allow us to postpone doomsday for a very long time.

3. ABSORBING KNOWLEDGE

3.1. Two Main Channels for Technology Transfers

There is no single factor that accounts for the remarkable success stories of the so-called East Asian tigers (i.e., Hong Kong, Taiwan, Singapore, South Korea, and China). But one aspect that these economies all have in common is their willingness and ability to *absorb* and adopt new technologies. Underlying the observed process of catch-up of these countries with high-income countries is the fact that it is generally easier to be a technological follower than a technological leader in the sense that it is presumably easier to learn how to *transfer* an existing new technology to a different country than it is to generate this technology in the first place.

While Griliches (1992) reports strong evidence on externalities in domestic R&D, the strength of international-research spillovers was more difficult to establish. However, in an important paper, Coe and Helpman (1995) construct measures of domestic and foreign R&D

capital stocks for a whole set of countries. The measures of foreign R&D are weighted averages of the domestic stocks of trade partners. They find that foreign R&D has a positive effect on domestic productivity and that the effect becomes more positive with the degree of trade openness. Hence, there is evidence of strong R&D spillovers, and there is also evidence that these are somewhat enhanced by *international trade.*[7]

There is more than one reason why international trade should increase the scope for cross-country knowledge spillovers. First, by engaging in the competitive market place of international trade, local companies *learn* to use state-of-the-art techniques and to produce goods that local consumers are willing to pay for. Also, when local consumers start buying modern high-quality imported foreign goods they start to demand the same quality from local firms, who then are pressured into modernizing. In other words, international trade fosters innovations by *increasing product market competition*. Finally, international trade allows a country to produce a specialized range of goods on a larger scale to meet a global demand while relying on imports to satisfy the local demand for other goods. Thus, international trade fosters innovations by allowing potential innovators, both in higher- and lower-income countries, to take advantage of *economies of scale*. That is, with large-scale production, firms more quickly acquire specialized knowledge of how to reduce production costs, and they also have more incentives to generate and implement cost-reducing innovations.

A second channel for cross-country technology transfers is *foreign direct investment* (FDI). FDI enables local workers to benefit from the know-how of foreign companies and to learn through practical experience how to become efficient managers and entrepreneurs; it enables local companies to learn by observing at close range how a successful company competes in the global economy.

The miracle economies of Southeast Asia have made extensive use of these two channels of technology transfers. Moreover, there is mounting evidence that the productivity-enhancing benefits of R&D activities in rich countries raises productivity in much poorer countries, but only to the extent that high- and low-income countries are open to international trade, foreign investment, and knowledge diffusion.

---

[7] However, see Keller (1998) for a more skeptical view on this.

In the process of catching up with high-income countries, poor countries that open themselves to international trade and FDI and who can thereby improve their access to foreign technologies may benefit not just from old innovations but also from the very latest ones. For example, one hurdle on the road to development is the creation of transportation and communication infrastructure. The information/communication revolution of recent years has reduced the costs of overcoming this hurdle by several orders of magnitude. Instead of building a dense network of costly telephone lines across rugged terrain and running wires to millions of houses, a country can connect its citizens with wireless phones, which have the added advantage of transportability. Similarly, no part of the world stands more to gain from biotechnological progress than Africa, which has been ravaged by AIDS and malaria in the last part of the 20th century, and where severe agricultural conditions enhance the payoff of new genetically designed seed and livestock varieties.

Yet some low-income countries may hesitate on fully opening up to trade and FDI; an important reason for such hesitation has to do with the threat of creative destruction – the fact that new goods, new processes, and new skills and occupations often make their old counterpart become obsolete – Hence, a potential conflict of interest that must somehow be resolved. The threat of creative destruction is what induces vested interests in every country to push for measures that would preserve the status quo against obsolescence – measures such as regulatory arrangements that favor incumbent firms, foreign ownership rules that protect domestically owned firms against foreign equity participation, import restrictions that protect domestic industries against international competition, banking laws that make it easier for established firms than start-ups to get finance, religious prohibitions that preserve old ways of life, national educational systems that maintain outdated curricula and teaching methods, and so forth. These measures offer security to individuals in an uncertain and changing world. But they also have a serious cost; by favoring the old over the new, they impede the technological change that the local country needs in order to catch up with richer countries. The example of Argentina during the past century is quite enlightening in this respect: once among the most prosperous in the world at the beginning of the 20th century, Argentina has now fallen behind as a result of tariff protections, state regulations, domestic ownership requirements, and paternalistic labor laws, all of which contributed to isolate this country from the world economy.

3.2. Facilitating Technology Transfers: Education and Infrastructure

To take advantage of technological progress generated elsewhere, a country must invest in education and in local public goods such as infrastructure. That education should enhance the creation and diffusion of new technological knowledge, and thereby speed up convergence with high-income countries, comes out clearly from the comparison between East Asian countries (for example South Korea, with an education policy that dates back to the independence war against Japan) and Latin America (e.g., Brazil or Mexico). Starting from comparable levels of gross domestic product GDP per capita in the early 1960s, the former countries in which education efforts have been more systematic have done much better in terms of absorbing Western technologies and thereby catching up with high-income countries.[8]

A possible interpretation of these findings is found in the Schumpeterian approach to education and growth developed by Nelson and Phelps (1966) and in which (i) growth is assumed to be positively affected by the rate of technological innovations and also by the rate of diffusion or adoption of existing technologies; and (ii) the *stock* of human capital affects these innovation and diffusion rates and, thereby, the country's rate of productivity growth. Evidence of such a complementarity between educational attainment and innovative activities comes out of microeconomic studies such as that by Bartel and Lichtenberg (1987), who found that "the relative demand for educated workers declines as the capital stock ages."[9]

The suggested complementarity between education and R&D activities has, in turn, interesting policy implications. First, it suggests that

---

[8] The comparison between Latin America and Southeast Asia also sheds interesting light on the relationship between growth and the *organization* of education in lower-income countries. In particular, the excessive emphasis on higher education and basic research at the expense of primary/secondary education in Latin American countries such as Mexico or Brazil may partly explain why these countries have underperformed in comparison to the East Asian tigers, where education has remained somewhat less elitist.

[9] In Section 3.3.2 we shall come back to the more theoretical aspects of the debate between the capital-based and the Schumpeterian approaches to education and growth.

policies aimed at encouraging innovative investments will also affect the relative demand for educated workers. In other words, governments can increase the average level of education not only directly through education policy but also indirectly by actively supporting domestic R&D activities. Conversely, government subsidies to education will increase the profitability of R&D activities, and thereby speed up technological progress in the country.

The fact that public support of domestic R&D should stimulate knowledge absorption and the catch-up process is also well illustrated in last year's World Bank report on knowledge and development. When describing the Green Revolution, undertaken in the early postwar period to create and disseminate new agricultural knowledge (e.g., the breeding of new seeds to increase factor productivity in agriculture), the report points to the key role played by domestic R&D policy in LDCs, in particular with the creation of national agriculture research organizations, largely financed with public funds, to develop second-generation varieties of seeds that would better adapt to the local environment. For example, as a result of this policy the number of new varieties of rice and corn doubled between 1966 and 1985.

Investments in infrastructure, both physical and institutional, have also been shown to play an important role in the process of technological catch-up by emerging market economies. For strong evidence on this, we refer to World Bank studies on infrastructure and also to the 1997 Transition Report published by the European Bank for Reconstruction and Development (EBRD).

There are again several reasons for why good infrastructure can stimulate technological innovation and diffusion. First, by reducing transportation costs, good transport and communication systems should increase the *mobility* of skilled workers across firms and industries. As argued by Lucas (1993), this in turn should result in a higher rate of technological innovation and diffusion in the various sectors of the economy.

Second, as argued in the EBRD Transition Report, infrastructure investments in transport and communication will reduce transaction costs and thereby increase market competition. Market competition in turn enhances innovations. For example, Aghion and Schankerman (1999) argue that infrastructure investments, which reduce transport and communication costs, also increase the market share of the most efficient firms and therefore encourage restructuring and innovations aimed at reducing costs.[10] The fact that product market competition enhances productivity growth is clearly shown in recent empirical work by Blundell et al. (1995) and Nickell (1996).

Market-enhancing infrastructure involves not only transportation and communication equipments, but also the provision of a legal, regulatory, financial, and political framework in which innovative entrepreneurship can flourish because the threat of fraud, the risks of expropriation, the scope for bureaucratic government interference, and the extent of credit-rationing have been minimized.

3.3. Cross-Country Convergence Analysis Revisited

An unfortunate prediction of the AK model of endogenous growth, where knowledge is treated like nothing more than capital, is that positive long-run growth is simply inconsistent with the possibility of cross-country convergence. Consider indeed two countries or regions, each of them governed by the same kind of dynamic equations as in sub-section 2.2. Either these two countries (regions) share the same fundamental characteristics (in terms of savings rate, depreciation rate, production technologies, etc.), in which case from the start these two economies will grow at the same rate, $g = sA_0 - \delta$, or these countries will have different characteristics or may be subject to stochastic shocks, in which case their growth paths should simply diverge over time. In contrast, the neoclassical model immediately implies that, everything else remaining equal, a richer country that has accumulated a larger stock of capital should grow more slowly than a poorer country with the same economic parameters but a lower capital stock. There, in fact, is strong evidence of a *convergence* pattern in per capita income, not only across regions with different starting points but similar economic characteristics (like between different states within the United States), but also between industrialized countries and emerging market economies, in particular in Southeast Asia (see Barro and Sala-i-Martín, 1995). This cross-country evidence on income differences has in turn been used to criticize endogenous growth theory as a whole.

Mankiw, Romer, and Weil (1992) – henceforth MRW – have led this attack while arguing that the neoclassical growth model with

---

[10] See also Aghion et al. (2001) for a Schumpeterian model where long-run growth is enhanced by market competition, the idea there being that innovation is a way to "escape competition."

exogenous technical progress and diminishing returns to capital (see Section 2.1) can explain most of the cross-country variation in output per capita. The problem with the traditional Solow model is that with capital as the only cumulable factor, and given that estimates of the co-efficient on capital lie in the range of 0.3 to 0.6, the implied convergence rate is much higher than the one estimated from cross-country regressions, being around 0.02. In order words, there seemed to be excessively strong diminishing returns to capital. MRW tried to solve this puzzle by introducing (unbounded) human capital accumulation on top of physical capital accumulation. The augmented Solow model then postulates a production function of the form $Y = K^\alpha H^\beta (AL)^{1-\alpha-\beta}$. The joint coefficient on physical and human capital, $\alpha + \beta$, is still less than one but necessarily greater than the estimated coefficient on capital. As a result, the returns to cumulable factors diminish, but only very slowly, and the implied convergence rate is therefore lowered.

In the next subsection[11] we will challenge MRW and argue that the evidence on cross-country convergence and income differences is more supportive of the Schumpeterian version of endogenous growth theory – in which knowledge creation results from innovations and cross-country convergence results from knowledge diffusion – than it is of neoclassical theory.

3.3.1. R&D Spillovers

In contrast to the neoclassical model where convergence is entirely driven by the diminishing return to capital assumption, convergence in the Schumpeterian model is driven by technological spillovers. That these spillovers should play an important role in explaining convergence had already been pointed out by various authors, including Helliwell and Chung (1991), Parente and Prescott (1994), and Eaton and Kortum (1996). We shall now consider a multi-country extension of the model in Section 2.3, in which countries are connected by R&D spillovers of the kind estimated by Coe and Helpman (1995); namely, we assume that an innovator from any country automatically moves to the worldwide leading-edge level of technology. This assumption in turn implies that a lagging country, where average productivity is lower than in the rest of the world, will make, on average, bigger innovations

---

[11] Based on Howitt (2000). See also Aghion and Howitt (1998, Chapters 1 and 12).

than other countries and, therefore, conditionally upon innovating, it will catch up with more advanced countries.[12]

This extended model is able (i) to explain conditional convergence without having to introduce (unbounded) human capital accumulation on top of physical capital accumulation like MRW; (ii) to explain "club convergence," that is, the fact that convergence is restricted to a sub-group of countries, namely those who are able and willing to invest in R&D; and (iii) to account for the observed positive correlation between cross-country differences in GDP per capita, and cross-country differences both in productivity and investment rates, particularly R&D intensity. Instead, by assuming that productivity differences across countries are uncorrelated with investment rates, MRW end up *over*-estimating the impact of increased capital on a country's steady-state level of per capita GDP because they attribute to capital accumulation something that should be attributed to productivity and R&D intensity.

More formally, we consider a world economy composed of m countries, indexed by $j \in \{1, 2, \ldots, m\}$. Each country produces according to the production technology specified in equation (13). The main difference lies in the assumption of *worldwide* technological spillovers; that is, at any date there is a worldwide leading-edge technology parameter $A^{\max}$,

$$A^{\max} = \max\{A_{ij}; i \in [0, 1], 1 \le j \le m\}, \tag{22}$$

where A_{ij} denotes the current productivity level in sector i of country j, we then assume that an innovation occurring in sector i of a country results in a new vintage of that country's intermediate input i, whose productivity parameter is equal to the current worldwide leading-edge level $A^{\max}$.

In each country, the innovation technology is the same as in the one-country model in sub-section 2.3, but now all innovating countries will grow in the long run at the same worldwide rate:

$$g = \frac{\dot{A}^{\max}}{A^{\max}} = \sum_{1 \le j \le m} \sigma_j \lambda_j n_j, \tag{23}$$

---

[12] The following formalization is borrowed from Howitt (2000). See also Aghion and Howitt (1998, Chapter 12) where convergence is instead driven by the assumption that the arrival rate parameter is an increasing function of the difference between the leading-edge productivity and the country's average productivity. The analysis remains otherwise identical to that reported in this section.

where the σ_j are non-negative spillover coefficients, λ_j measures the productivity of R&D in country j, and n_j measures the R&D intensity in country j.

Let A denote current average productivity in a particular country (we omit the sub-index j for notational simplicity). This parameter will grow over time as a result of domestic innovations, each of which moves the sector in which it occurs up to the current leading-edge level A^{max}. Since innovations are equally likely to occur in any sector of the domestic economy, average productivity growth is governed by the differential equation

$$\dot{A} = \lambda n (A^{max} - A). \tag{24}$$

In particular, a country with a higher rate of innovations λn will be more productive on average because a larger fraction of its sectors will have recently innovated and, thereby, moved their productivity parameters up to the current leading edge. Now, let $a \equiv A/A^{max}$ denote the domestic country's average productivity relative to the leading edge. Dividing both sides of the preceding differential equation by A^{max} and using the fact that $g = \dot{A}^{max}/A^{max}$, we obtain the following differential equation for a:

$$\dot{a} = \lambda n (1 - a) - ag. \tag{25}$$

This equation describes the mechanism whereby knowledge transfers generate convergence to the global growth rate. An increase in R&D will temporarily raise productivity growth, but as the gap $(1 - a)$ narrows between the country's average productivity and the worldwide leading edge, innovations will raise productivity by less and less, which in turn will slow down the growth rate of the country's average productivity. This equation, together with the dynamic equation for capital accumulation and the research arbitrage equation (15), which determines the equilibrium R&D intensity as a function of the capital stock, will fully characterize the dynamic evolution of this multi-country economy starting from initial values a_0 and k_0.

Assuming the same constant savings rate s for all countries, and letting $k = K/AL = K/A$, capital accumulation in each country j is simply governed by the following equation:

$$\dot{k} = sk^\alpha - \left(\delta + \frac{\dot{A}}{A}\right)k = sk^\alpha - (\delta + \lambda n(a^{-1} - 1))k. \tag{26}$$

This is identical to the equation for capital accumulation in the neo-classical model, except that the rate of technological progress $\dot{A}/A$ is now endogenous.

The multi-country model is now fully specified and we can use it to vindicate our three claims, respectively, on club convergence, on accounting for the positive correlation between per capita income levels and investment rates/productivity/R&D intensities across countries, and on convergence rates.

Club convergence When deriving the research arbitrage equation in section 2.3, we have implicitly restricted the analysis to the case where the equilibrium research intensity n is strictly positive. More generally, the research arbitrage condition is expressed as

$$1 - \psi \geq \lambda \frac{\tilde{\pi}(k)}{r + \lambda n}; n \geq 0,$$

with at least one equality. In particular, a country j with very low R&D productivity λ_j and/or low R&D subsidy ψ, and/or low appropriability of innovation rents (i.e., low $\tilde{\pi}(k)$ for given k), or high interest rate r, will remain in a no-innovation/no-growth trap with $n = 0$ in steady state; on the other hand, countries with higher R&D productivity, higher rent appropriability, and lower interest rates will undertake R&D and thereby converge to the common growth rate g. Hence, only "club" members will converge, whereas the poorest countries will remain on the sidewalk in the absence of public and/or foreign aid.

Cross-country regressions The steady-state corresponding to the differential Equations (25) and (26) is simply given by

$$a = \frac{\lambda n}{g + \lambda n} \tag{27}$$

and

$$sk^{\alpha - 1} = \delta + g, \tag{28}$$

where the equilibrium R&D intensity n is determined by the aforementioned research arbitrage condition. Now, using the latter equation to substitute for k, and re-expressing per capita income as

$$\frac{Y}{L} = ak^{\alpha} A^{\max}, \tag{29}$$

we obtain the steady-state equation

$$\ln \frac{Y}{L} = \ln A^{\max} + \ln a + \frac{\alpha}{1-\alpha}(\ln s - \ln(\delta + g)). \tag{30}$$

This equation is almost identical to that by MRW, except for the additional term "$\ln a$". However, unlike MRW, the residual term $\Omega = (\ln A^{\max} + \ln a)$ is positively correlated with the regressor $(\ln s - \ln(\delta + g))$; in particular, countries with a higher savings rate s are also those countries that do more R&D and therefore display a higher ratio between the average and the leading-edge levels of productivity in steady state, i.e., a higher level of a. Ignoring this correlation in turn leads MRW to a biased estimate of the capital coefficient α and, more specifically, to overestimate the direct contribution of capital to growth.

Convergence rates   From equation (24) we immediately get

$$\frac{\dot{A}}{A} = \lambda n(a^{-1} - 1). \tag{31}$$

In other words, countries that are closer to the leading edge should experience lower spillovers and therefore lower rates of productivity growth. Unlike MRW, we do not need to introduce (unbounded) human capital accumulation on top of physical capital accumulation in order to reconcile the observed evidence about the convergence rate with that on the capital coefficient.

3.3.3. The Nelson–Phelps Approach to Human Capital

The preceding discussion has shown that knowledge spillovers provide an alternative explanation of convergence to the augmented Solow model of MRW. Yet a large body of empirical evidence has shown that education measured by past education attainment has been growth-enhancing, just as MRW predict.[13] In this sub-section we will argue that technological spillovers are consistent with the presence of education variables in convergence equations once we take into account the Nelson–Phelps approach to human capital.

A possible interpretation of the finding that education is positively correlated with growth is found by Lucas (1988), where only the *unbounded accumulation* of human capital, not its current stock, is meant

---

[13] See Temple (1999) for a review.

to sustain growth. Lucas maintains that both physical and human capital are standard inputs in production, and that they both exhibit diminishing returns, although the production function is characterized by constant returns to these two types of capital together. Investments in human capital prevent the marginal product of physical capital from falling as the latter grows, and vice versa, thus providing the necessary incentives for perpetual investment in education and machinery. As a result, output growth is driven by the unbounded accumulation of the two types of capital.

This argument is to be contrasted with the Schumpeterian approach to education and growth by Nelson and Phelps (1966), discussed in Sub-section 3.2.1, where growth can be positive even if human capital accumulation is bounded. The crucial difference lies in the factor that is assumed to be accumulated without bound: is it knowledge or human capital? As our librarians know, knowledge can be accumulated seemingly without limit, requiring simply more space for the books, journals, or computers that store information. Human capital, on the other hand, is *embodied* in individuals. This implies that when the individual disappears the knowledge and skills that she acquired over her lifetime also disappear. Hence, as each generation is born, its members have to be re-educated and thus cannot build upon the human capital accumulated by the previous generation, even though the former can benefit from the knowledge that the latter created.[14]

The question that arises, then, is whether the more realistic premises of the Schumpeterian model, where human capital accumulation is bounded and knowledge creation is unbounded, yield predictions that can be reconciled with the evidence on education and growth. We now follow De la Fuente (1995) and Desdoigts (2000) and show that, if the stock human capital is assumed to be a determinant of a country's absorption capacity, then the aforementioned Schumpeterian model with cross-country knowledge spillovers will lead to a convergence equation equivalent to that implied by the neoclassical model with human capital. In other words, the evidence on the growth-enhancing role of human capital does not seriously challenge the Schumpeterian approach advocated in this chapter, and in particular it does not provide support for growth models with unbounded human capital accumulation.

---

[14] That human capital accumulation cannot be assumed to be unbounded like physical capital accumulation has been well argued by Young (1991) in his work on learning by doing.

Consider a standard Cobb–Douglas production function, $Y = K^\alpha (AL)^{1-\alpha}$. Let k be the stock of capital per unit of effective labor, so that output per worker can be expressed as

$$y = Ak^\alpha. \tag{32}$$

Output growth is then the result of technological change and capital accumulation. With a constant saving rate, capital accumulation is governed by the equation

$$\dot{k} = sk^\alpha - \left(\delta + \frac{\dot{A}}{A}\right) k. \tag{33}$$

Following Nelson and Phelps, suppose that technological progress depends on both the gap between the domestic and the leading-edge level of productivity and on the absorption capacity of the country, ϕ. This absorption capacity is in turn assumed to be an increasing function of the stock of human capital. That is,

$$\dot{A} = \phi(h)(A^{\max} - A), \tag{34}$$

with $\phi(0) = 0$ and $\phi'(h) > 0$. It is now clear that the evolution of the technological gap, $a \equiv A/A^{\max}$, is governed by the following differential equation for a,

$$\dot{A} = \phi(h)(1 - a) - ag, \tag{35}$$

and that it will converge to the equilibrium gap

$$a^* = \frac{\phi(h)}{g + \phi(h)}. \tag{36}$$

Differentiating the production function, log-linearizing around the steady-state capital stock k^*, and using Equation (33), we can express the rate of output growth as

$$\frac{\dot{y}}{y} = \frac{\dot{A}}{A} - \beta(\ln y - \ln A) - \alpha(\beta \ln k^* - \phi(h)(\ln a^* - \ln a)). \tag{37}$$

Substituting for the steady-state capital stock k^* and using Equations (35) and (36) for the technology gap, we have the following convergence equation:

$$\frac{\dot{y}}{y} = g + \beta\left(\ln A_0^{\max} + gt - \ln y_0\right) + \frac{\alpha}{1-\alpha}\beta(\ln s - \ln(\delta + g))$$

$$+ \beta \ln \frac{\phi(h)}{g + \phi(h)} - \beta\left[\ln \frac{\phi(h)}{g + \phi(h)} - \ln a\right]\left(\frac{\phi(h)}{\delta + g} - 1\right)e^{-\phi(h)t}. \quad (38)$$

Once again, the resulting equation is almost identical to the convergence equation by MRW, except for the last term. It predicts convergence conditional on, among other things, the stock of human capital. However, in contrast to the augmented Solow model of MRW, education does not affect growth through its rate of accumulation but through its impact on the country's capacity to absorb knowledge spillovers. The stock of human capital affects growth in two ways. First, the rate of growth of output per worker is a decreasing function of the equilibrium technological gap, which is itself a decreasing function of the stock of human capital. Second, for a given stock of human capital, the rate of growth is higher the greater is the distance between the current technological gap and the steady-state one. That is, the Nelson–Phelps approach predicts that we should observe an interaction between the stock of human capital and relative technology levels. What does the evidence tell us?

3.3.4. Neoclassical Convergence versus Technological Catch-Up

Having shown that the Schumpeterian approach to endogenous growth can be reconciled with the evidence on cross-country per capita income levels and growth rates, we can ask ourselves whether the existing empirical evidence is more supportive of the neoclassical or the Schumpeterian convergence approach.

In their paper, MRW claim that around 80% of the international variation in per capita incomes can be explained by three variables: population growth, and the rates of investment in physical and human capital. If this is the case, there is not much left to be explained by differences in technology levels. However, Klenow and Rodríguez-Clare (1997) point out a major problem of these results, namely that MRW use a human capital measure that only captures differences in secondary schooling. Ignoring primary schooling implies an exaggeration of the cross-country variation in human capital investment rates and, consequently, leads to an overestimation of the contribution of this variable to growth. Klenow and Rodríguez-Clare find that when primary schooling is included in the measure of human capital, the augmented Solow model can in fact only explain about 50% of the variation in incomes. Differences in technology could then, in principle, account for the rest.

Another problem with the MRW type of approach is that changes in human capital accumulation seem to explain little of the variation in changes in output, as found by Benhabib and Spiegel (1994) and Pritchett (2001). Benhabib and Spiegel (1994) in fact provide the first serious test of the Nelson–Phelps approach at the macroeconomic level. Particularly interesting in Benhabib and Spiegel's analysis is their implicit refutation of both the neoclassical and the AK approaches, in which education only contributes to the accumulation of (human) capital, and where growth is entirely driven by capital accumulation. More specifically, Benhabib and Spiegel (1994) use a growth accounting framework to try to disentangle the contributions of human capital and education to growth. Whereas past education attainment (as a measure of the current stock of human capital) is found to be essentially *uncorrelated* with growth if one uses an augmented Solow model where human capital is nothing but an ordinary input in the aggregate production function, the effect of past education attainment levels on current growth rates becomes *significant* if one follows the more Schumpeterian approach to education and growth developed by Nelson and Phelps (1966).

In a recent paper, Desdoigts (2000) specifies a general convergence equation that incorporates both the neoclassical and the Schumpeterian model, along the lines of Equation (38). Growth is thus, in principle, determined by both the accumulation of human and physical capital and by technological spillovers, where the capacity to absorb these spillovers is determined by either human capital stocks or investment rates. Using this unified framework it is possible to estimate growth equations and let the data choose between the various nested models. Desdoigts finds that, as far as education is concerned, the MRW specification can be improved upon if a country's absorption capacity is proxied by human capital measures. Moreover, the explanatory power of the model improves substantially when the technology gap term is interacted with a country's share of equipment investment in output. He then undertakes an interesting exercise: taking 1960 as the initial point, Desdoigts calculates the world distribution of incomes in 1985

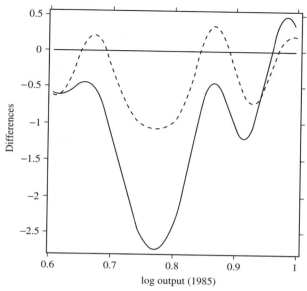

Figure 1. The world distribution of incomes. Prediction errors from the neo-classical (—) and Schumpeterian (- - -) models.

using the two estimated models, and compares it to the actual distribution of incomes in 1985. The results are striking. The income levels obtained from the MRW model bear little resemblance to those that actually prevailed, while the distribution generated by the technological catch-up model exhibits the same double hump that we observe in the actual distribution. Figure 1 presents the difference in densities between the actual and the two simulated distributions. It clearly implies a much more satisfactory performance of the Schumpeterian approach (dotted line) than of the neoclassical model (solid line).

4. CONCLUSIONS

The lesson that we have learned from our discussion is that innovation drives global growth and convergence. The first important implication of the Schumpeterian approach with technology transfers is that, in contrast to the neoclassical framework, convergence is global rather than only conditional. All countries with positive R&D levels will converge to parallel growth paths, with the same positive growth rate, while other countries will stagnate. We have argued that countries differ in per capita income not only because of differences in capital stocks but also because of differences in productivity. The Schumpeterian model is then not only consistent with existing cross-country evidence on growth rates, but also accounts for the cross-country differences in productivity levels that recent research has shown to be quite large.

The second crucial implication of Schumpeterian endogenous growth is that there is, in principle, a trade-off between creating and diffusing knowledge. The importance of such a trade-off seems to be accepted both by academic economists and by the popular press, as we could see in the recent claim by Bill Gates that competition and antitrust legislation are detrimental for innovation and growth. This argument becomes particularly important when we consider open economies and the role of international spillovers. We have argued that openness, in the form of both international trade and FDI, is crucial for the absorption of knowledge. The question is then whether it is also good for the creation of knowledge. It is often argued that this is not the case; international trade enhances imitation and thus erodes the rents that can be obtained by domestic innovators. There is nevertheless an important counter-argument – the idea that innovation is a way to escape competition. If openness subjects domestic producers to increased competition and thus reduces their profitability, it will consequently provide the incentives for R&D investments in order to improve their technological advantage and hence recoup their profit level.

Opening up to international trade or allowing for FDIs, however, will remain of little use for less-developed economies if there is not a willingness of incumbent innovators in rich countries to partly overcome their own creative destruction dilemma and diffuse their innovations to the poorer countries. This means that, unlike in the neoclassical model, the legal environment is crucial for growth and convergence. Can international patent protection overcome the Schumpeterian trade-off and both protect ownership rights and enhance diffusion? Michael Kremer (2000) has recently put forward a proposal that aims at attaining this. The basic idea is to create an *innovation purchase fund*. The fund would buy patents for new goods or technologies from private innovators and would then put them in the public domain, thus ensuring an adequate diffusion. The crucial issue is how to determine the price at which the patent is purchased. Kremer's suggestion is to establish an initial price for a particular innovation and have the price rise according to a preannounced schedule until the innovation is actually developed. This is similar to an auction system procedure: if nobody is willing to produce the good at a low price, the fund tries a higher price until it is developed.

The role of human capital in the growth process also questions the extent of the trade-off between creating and absorbing knowledge. We have argued that, in the Schumpeterian model, human capital is a major determinant of a country's capacity to absorb knowledge spillovers. Education policies thus play a crucial role in technological catch-up. A second important feature of human capital is that it is an essential input in the creation of new knowledge. In fact, it is often argued that only when a country has accumulated enough human capital can it move from being an imitator to being an innovator. This implies that policies aimed at increasing a country's absorption capacity and the diffusion of knowledge will also generate the necessary conditions for that economy to eventually start creating knowledge itself.

REFERENCES

Aghion, Philippe, and Peter Howitt (1992), "A Model of Growth Through Creative Destruction," *Econometrica* 60: 323–51.

Aghion, Philippe, and Peter Howitt (1998), *Endogenous Growth Theory*, MIT Press, Cambridge, MA.

Aghion, Philippe, and Mark Schankerman (1999), "Competition, Entry and the Social Returns to Infrastructure in Transition Economies," *Economics of Transition* 7: 79–101.

Aghion, Philippe, Christopher Harris, Peter Howitt, and John Vickers (2001), "Competition, Imitation and Growth with Step-by-Step Innovation," *Review of Economic Studies* 68: 467–92.

Barro, Robert, and Xavier Sala-i-Martín (1995), *Economic Growth*, McGraw-Hill, New York.

Bartel, A., and F. Lichtenberg (1987), "The Comparative Advantage of Educated Workers in Implementing New Technology," *Review of Economics and Statistics*, 69: 1–11.

Benhabib, J., and M. M. Spiegel (1994), "The Role of Human Capital in Economic Development: Evidence from Cross-Country Data," *Journal of Monetary Economics*, 34: 143–73.

Blundell, Richard, Rachel Griffith, and John Van Reenen (1995), "Dynamic Count Data Models of Technological Innovation," *Economic Journal* 105: 333–44.

Coe, David T., and Elhanan Helpman (1995), "International R&D Spillovers," *European Economic Review* 39(5): 859–97.

Dasgupta, Partha (1994), "Optimal Development and the Idea of Net National Product," in I. Goldin and L. A. Winders (eds.), *The Economics of Sustainable Development*, Cambridge University Press, Cambridge.

De la Fuente, Angel (1995), "Catch-Up, Growth and Convergence in the OECD," Center for Economic Policy Research Discussion Paper No. 1274.

Desdoigts, Alain (2000), "Neoclassical Convergence versus Technological Catch-Up: A Contribution for Reaching a Consensus," mimeo, Universite d'Evry.

Eaton, Jonathan, and Samuel Kortum (1996). "Trade in Ideas: Patenting and Productivity in the OECD," *Journal of International Economics* 40(3–4): 251–78.

Frankel, M. (1962), "The Production Function in Allocation and Growth: A Synthesis," *American Economic Review* 62: 995–1022.

Griliches, Zvi. (1992), "The Search for R&D Spillovers," *Scandinavian Journal of Economics* 94: 92–116.

Grossman, G. M. and E. Helpman (1991), "Quality Ladders and Product Cycles." *Quarterly Journal of Economics*, 106: 557–86.

Helliwell, John F., and Alan Chung (1991), "Macroeconomic Convergence: International Transmission of Growth and Technical Progress," in Peter Hooper and J. David Richardson (eds.), *International Economic Transactions: Issues in Measurement and Empirical Research*. NBER Studies in Income and Wealth, Vol. 55, The University of Chicago Press, Chicago, pp. 388–436.

Howitt, Peter (2000), "Endogenous Growth and Cross-Country Income Differences," *American Economic Review*, 90: 829–46.

Keller W. (1998), "Are International R&D Spillovers Trade-related? Analyzing Spillovers Among Randomly Matched Trade Partners," *European Economic Review*, 42: 1469–81.

Klenow, Peter J., and Andrés Rodríguez-Clare (1997), "The Neoclassical Revival in Growth Economics: Has it Gone too Far?" in Ben Bernanke and Julio Rotemberg (eds.), *NBER Macroeconomics Annual*, MIT Press, Cambridge, MA, pp. 73–103.

Kortum, S. (1997), "Research, Patenting, and Technological Change," *Econometrica*, 65(6): 1389–1481.

Kremer, Michael (2000), "A Purchase Fund for New Vaccines: Rationale and a Proposed Design," mimeo, Harvard University, Cambridge, MA.

Lucas, Robert E. (1988), "On the Mechanics of Economic Development," *Journal of Monetary Economics* 22(1): 3–42.

Lucas, Robert E. (1993), "Making a Miracle," *Econometrica* 61(2): 251–72.

Mankiw, N. Gregory, David Romer, and David N. Weil (1992), "A Contribution to the Empirics of Economic Growth," *Quarterly Journal of Economics* 107(2): 407–37.

Nelson, R. R., and E. S. Phelps (1966). "Investment in Humans, Technological Diffusion, and Economic Growth," *American Economic Review* 61: 69–75.

Nickell, Stephen (1996), "Competition and Corporate Performance," *Journal of Political Economy* 104: 724–46.

Parente, Stephen L., and Edward C. Prescott (1994), "Technology Adoption and Growth," *Journal of Political Economy* 102(2): 298–321.

Pritchett, Lant (2001). "Where Has All the Education Gone?" *World Bank Economic Review* 15: 367–91.

Romer and M. Paul (1986), "Increasing Returns and Long Run Growth," *Journal of Political Economy* 94(5): 1002–37.

Romer and M. Paul (1990), "Endogenous Technological Change," *Journal of Political Economy* 98(5): 71–102.

Sergestrom, P. S., T. Anant, and E. Dinopoulos (1990), "Innovation, Imitation and Economic Growth," *American Economic Review* 80: 1077–92.

Solow and M. Robert (1956), "A Contribution to the Theory of Economic Growth," *Quarterly Journal of Economics* 70: 65–94.

Swan, T. W. (1956), "Economic Growth and Capital Accumulation," *Economic Record* 32: 34–361.

Temple, Jonathan (1999), "The New Growth Evidence," *Journal of Economic Literature*, 37: 112–156.

Young, Alwyn (1991), "Learning by Doing and the Dynamic Effects of International Trade," *Quarterly Journal of Economics* 106(2): 369–406.

PART TWO

Statistical Issues in Growth and Dynamics

4

Delinearizing the Neoclassical Convergence Model

Steve Dowrick

DELINEARIZING THE NEOCLASSICAL CONVERGENCE MODEL

The empirical analysis of economic growth has become a major international research program, fueled in part by vigorous debate between proponents of models of endogenous growth, based on the accumulation of knowledge and ideas, and the defenders of the neoclassical growth model established by Trevor Swan and Robert Solow in their seminal papers, both published in 1956.

A central tenet of the neoclassical tradition is that the accumulation of factors for use in production, whether physical capital or intangible capital in the form of education and skills, is subject to a strict version of the "Law" of diminishing returns: namely, the Inada condition that the marginal product of capital tends toward zero as the stock of capital increases. This condition implies that capital accumulation cannot drive long-run growth in labor productivity or income per person, which must instead come from labor-augmenting technological progress. In the short run, however, the rate of capital accumulation influences the speed of transition from any historically determined starting point to the economy's steady state. As a general rule, the speed of transitional growth is decreasing in the ratio of current to steady-state capital intensity. Given common technology, differences in capital intensity translate into differences in labor productivity. It follows that, if we control for differences in the determinants of steady state, countries with low labor productivity will exhibit faster growth than countries with high labor productivity. This is the "conditional convergence" prediction of the neoclassical growth model.

By way of contrast, the first generation of modern models of endogenous growth, such as Romer (1990) and Lucas (1988), suggest

83

that country-specific characteristics that determine the rate of accumulation of knowledge and/or skill will also determine each country's stable long-run growth rate. The countries with the highest growth-promoting characteristics would forever grow faster than other countries. In such a world we would expect to observe unconditional divergence of productivity and living standards. Evidence that such stark divergence has not occurred has been important to the arguments of neoclassical counter-revolutionists such as Jones (1995).

The contrasting predictions of endogenous growth models and the neoclassical model have re-ignited interest in empirical tests of the conditional convergence prediction of the neoclassical model. Mankiw, Romer, and Weil (1992) – henceforth MRW – have popularized a first-order approximation to the dynamics of the Solow–Swan growth model, yielding a specification that is assumed to be linear, allowing ordinary least squares (OLS) estimation of the rate of convergence. They also developed an augmented model that allows for the accumulation of human as well as physical capital. Many subsequent empirical studies have used variations of the MRW specification in cross-country, panel, and time-series analyses of growth. The Social Science Citation Index reports over three hundred citations of this seminal paper.

Here we demonstrate that the first-order approximation to Solow–Swan transitional dynamics is nonlinear in the context of cross-country regressions because the rate of convergence varies across countries. Moreover, the standard regression specification is over-identified. Accordingly, we report nonlinear estimation of the standard model in order to assess the magnitude of the bias that results from the MRW misspecification.

Since we are required to use non-linear regression techniques to estimate the first-order approximation, it is natural to wonder whether there is any need to approximate the dynamics of the model in the first place. So we derive the exact expression for the transitional growth path of the nonaugmented model in order to obtain further nonlinear regression estimates.

THE FIRST-ORDER APPROXIMATION TO THE TRANSITIONAL DYNAMICS OF THE SOLOW–SWAN MODEL

MRW approximate the rate of growth in the vicinity of the steady state of the Solow–Swan model, taking the first-order Taylor approximation to the growth rate of output per unit of effective labor as a function of the logarithm of output per unit of effective labor. They assume that labor-augmenting technology, A_t, is common across all countries and grows at a common rate g. Production of the single good exhibits constant returns to scale and constant elasticities with respect to the inputs: physical capital, K_t, and effective labor, $A_t L_t$ (and, in the augmented model, human capital). The output elasticities are assumed to be constant across countries and across time. Capital depreciates at a constant proportional rate d that is also common across countries and time. The exogenous variables in the model are the ratio of investment to output, s_i, and the growth rate of the labor input, n_i, which are assumed to be constant over time but to vary exogenously across countries.

I set out here the steps required to derive the MRW specification in the case of the standard model with only physical capital. Subscript t indexes time and subscript i indexes countries. Output and capital per effective worker are denoted in lower case: y and k.

$$Y_{it} = K_{it}^{\alpha}(A_t L_{it})^{1-\alpha}, \quad L_{it} = L_{i0}e^{n_i t}, \quad A_t = A_0 e^{gt}, \quad 0 < \alpha < 1 \quad (1)$$

$$y_{it} \equiv \frac{Y_{it}}{A_t L_{it}}, \quad k_{it} \equiv \frac{K_{it}}{A_i L_{it}} \quad \Rightarrow \quad y_{it} = k_{it}^{\alpha} \quad (2)$$

$$\Delta_i \equiv (n_i + g + \delta). \quad (3)$$

The rate of capital dilution per effective worker is defined as Δ_i in Equation (3). It is straightforward to derive both the rate of change (denoted by a dot) of capital per effective worker and the proportional growth rate (denoted by a hat) as

$$\frac{dk_{it}}{dt} \equiv \dot{k}_{it} = s_i k_{it}^{\alpha} - \Delta_i k_{it} \quad (4)$$

$$\Rightarrow \frac{\dot{k}_{it}}{k_{it}} \equiv \hat{k}_{it} = s_i k_{it}^{\alpha-1} - \Delta_i. \quad (5)$$

The fact that the exponent on k in Equation (5) is strictly negative implies that the rate of growth of capital intensity, k, declines monotonically toward zero as k approaches its steady-state level, k^*, from below.

Defining steady-state capital and output per effective worker to be stationary,

$$k_i^* = [s_i/\Delta_i]^{\frac{1}{1-\alpha}}, \quad y^* = [s_i/\Delta_i]^{\frac{\alpha}{1-\alpha}}. \quad (6)$$

Substitution of Equations (2) and (6) into equation (5) gives the instantaneous rate of growth of output per effective worker as a nonlinear function of its level:

$$\hat{y}_{it} = \alpha \Delta_i \left[(y_i^*/y_{it})^{1-\alpha/\alpha} - 1 \right]. \tag{7}$$

MRW linearize (or, more accurately, log-linearize) this relationship using the first-order Taylor expansion around the steady state with respect to $\log(y_t)$:

$$\hat{y}_{it}[\log y_{it}] \cong \hat{y}_{it}[\log(y_i^*)] + \left. \frac{d(\hat{y}_{it})}{d \log(y_{it})} \right|_{y^*} (\log y_{it} - \log y_i^*). \tag{8}$$

The first term on the right-hand side is zero by definition of steady state, y^*. Differentiation of Equation (7) with respect to $\log(y)$ gives

$$\frac{d\hat{y}_{it}}{d \log y_{it}} = -(1-\alpha)\Delta_i (y_i^*/y_{it})^{1-\alpha/\alpha}. \tag{9}$$

Evaluating this expression at the steady state, substituting into Equation (8), and writing out the capital dilution term in full gives the first-order approximation to the instantaneous rate of growth as a function of the distance from steady state:

$$\hat{y}_{it} \cong -(1-\alpha)(n_i + g + \delta)(\log y_{it} - \log y_i^*). \tag{10}$$

The product of the first two terms in parentheses is defined by MRW as the convergence rate λ. We note that it is actually a country-specific parameter, λ_i:

$$\lambda_i \equiv (1-\alpha)(n_i + g + d). \tag{11}$$

This approximate rate of convergence to steady state is constant as long as rates of depreciation, population growth, and technology growth are constant. In the MRW model these factors are indeed assumed to be constant over time *within each country*. It is not legitimate, however, to treat convergence as a constant *across countries*. The rate of convergence is a function of population growth, which varies significantly from country to country. Higher rates of population growth imply faster convergence, with the half-life of convergence to steady state being $\log 2/\lambda$. If, for example, $\alpha = 0.4$ and $(g + d) = 0.05$, then a country with zero population growth will converge toward steady-state output at an annual rate of 3%, with a half-life of 23 years. A country with population growth of 4% per year will converge on steady state at an annual rate of 5.4%, with a half-life of just 13 years.

For empirical purposes we want to convert Equation (10) from an instantaneous growth rate into an expression for growth over a discrete period. Integration allows us to express the growth rate over T years as

$$\log \frac{y_{iT}}{y_{i0}} = (1 - e^{-\lambda_i T}) \log \frac{y_i^*}{y_{i0}}. \qquad (12)$$

Since effective labor, y, is unobservable, we derive the growth of output per worker Y/L by adding the exogenous rate of labor-augmenting technical progress, g, and substituting for y^* from Equation (6):

$$\log \frac{(Y/L)_{iT}}{(Y/L)_{i0}} = (1 - e^{-\lambda_i T}) \frac{\alpha}{1 - \alpha} \log \frac{s_i}{n_i + g + d}$$
$$- (1 - e^{-\lambda_i T}) \log (Y/L)_{i0} + (1 - e^{-\lambda_i T}) \log A_0 + g T. \qquad (13)$$

The augmented version of this model includes human capital as well as physical capital, resulting in an additional parameter, the elasticity of output with respect to human capital. The ratio of investment in human capital to gross domestic product is assumed to be an exogenous constant and the depreciation of human capital is assumed to be the same as that for physical capital. This results in the augmented MRW growth equation, which is similar to Equation (13) with the country-specific convergence parameter now defined as $\lambda_i \equiv (1 - \alpha - \beta)(n_i + g + d)$. For the purpose of this chapter, however, we shall work with the basic model since the problems arising out of the mis-specified cross-country regressions are the same for both models.

In estimating Equation (13), MRW make a number of explicit assumptions:

- Rates of technical progress and capital depreciation, g and d, are exogenous, constant across countries, and sum to 0.05.
- The production parameter α and the initial technology level A_0 are constant across countries.
- Investment rates, s_i, and population growth, n_i, vary across countries but are constant over time within each country.
- Investment rates and population growth are exogenous variables, uncorrelated with shocks to growth.

While not unusual in the empirical growth literature, these are strong assumptions.[1] For the purposes of this chapter, however, we maintain the aforementioned assumptions. Our focus is on two further assumptions that are not explicit in the MRW paper. They are clearly implied, however, by the fact that MRW treat Equation (13) as a relationship that can be estimated by OLS with an intercept term and two right-hand-side variables: the log of initial labor productivity and the log investment ratio. In Tables IV to VI, MRW report parameter estimates for regressions of the following form (in some cases augmented by human capital):

$$\log \frac{(Y/L)_{iT}}{(Y/L)_{i0}} = \beta_0 + \beta_1 \log(Y/L)_{i0} + \beta_2 \log \frac{s_i}{n_i + \overline{g} + \overline{d}} + \varepsilon_i, \quad (14)$$

where the over-bars on g and d indicate that numerical values are imposed.

Comparison of Equation (14) with Equation (13) yields the following interpretation of the regression parameters:

$$
\begin{aligned}
&\text{i)} \quad \beta_0 = (1 - e^{-\lambda_i T}) \log A_0 + \overline{g}T \\
&\text{ii)} \quad \beta_1 = -(1 - e^{-\lambda_i T}) \\
&\text{iii)} \quad \beta_2 = (1 - e^{-\lambda_i T})\frac{\alpha}{1 - \alpha} \\
&\text{given} \quad \lambda_i \equiv (1 - \alpha)(n_i + \overline{g} + \overline{d}).
\end{aligned}
\quad (15)
$$

The use of OLS to estimate Equation (14) implies that the parameters β_0, β_1, and β_2 are constants, but inspection of Equations (15) highlights two critical errors that are implicit in this procedure:

a) the term λ_i is treated as a constant across countries; and
b) the three β parameters can be estimated independently.

Neither of these assumptions is valid. The term λ_i is a function of population growth, which varies across countries. Furthermore, there are only two exogenous parameters, A_0 and α, to be estimated. The MRW growth equation is not only non-linear in the context of cross-country regressions, it is also over-identified.

---

[1] A number of studies have found evidence to reject the exogeneity of rates of investment (e.g., Brander and Dowrick, 1994; Barro and Sala-i-Martín, 1995). Other studies have rejected the hypothesis of common rates of technical progress (e.g., Lee et al. 1997).

DERIVING THE EXACT DYNAMICS OF
THE SOLOW–SWAN MODEL

Implicit in the MRW approach is the assumption that a first-order approximation to the transitional dynamics of the Solow–Swan model yields a linear regression equation. This approach would be valid if applied to a time series of growth rates for a country where population growth is constant. It is clearly invalid when applied to a cross section of countries where annual average growth rates of the labor force vary substantially – from 0.3% in the United Kingdom to 4.3% in the Ivory Coast.

Having demonstrated that estimation of the first-order approximation actually requires the use of nonlinear regression techniques, it is natural to ask why we should use the approximation in the first place. We are able to find an exact solution to the growth dynamics in the case where there is only one type of capital being accumulated. Starting again with the capital accumulation equation, and dropping the country subscripts for the moment, $dk/dt \equiv k = sk^{\alpha} - \Delta k$, we apply the Bernoulli transformation:

$$k_t^{-\alpha} k_t = s - \Delta k_t^{1-\alpha}. \tag{16}$$

Defining $x_t \equiv k_t^{1-\alpha}$, differentiation of both sides and substitution into Equation (16) yields a differential equation that is linear in x_t:

$$\frac{dx_t}{dt} = (1 - \alpha)(s - \Delta x_t). \tag{17}$$

Integration, with a constant of integration, c, yields

$$x_t = ce^{-(1-\alpha)\Delta t} + s/\Delta. \tag{18}$$

Expressing this in terms of the path of output, y_t, by inversion of the production function, and evaluating the constant of integration at time $t = 0$, gives the following result:

$$y_t^{(1-\alpha)/\alpha} = e^{-(1-\alpha)\Delta t} y_0^{(1-\alpha)/\alpha} + (1 - e^{-(1-\alpha)\Delta t})s/\Delta. \tag{19}$$

Converting to observable units, Y/L, gives the exact growth rate of labor productivity in country i between time 0 and T as

$$\log \frac{(Y/L)_{iT}}{(Y/L)_{i0}} = gT + \frac{\alpha}{1-\alpha} \log \left[e^{-\lambda_i T} + \frac{(1 - e^{-\lambda_i T})s_i}{n_i + g + d} \left(\frac{Y_{i0}}{A_0 L_{i0}} \right)^{1-\alpha/\alpha} \right]. \tag{20}$$

where the convergence parameter is again $\lambda_i = (1 - \alpha)(n_i + g + d)$. This exact expression can be contrasted with the first-order approximation (13).

LINEAR AND NONLINEAR ESTIMATION METHODS

We investigate the implications of the MRW mis-specification using their original data set. The variables are the growth of real output per worker, physical investment rates, and population growth averaged over the period 1960–85 for 98 non-OPEC countries. Descriptive statistics are given in Table 1.

The first column of figures in Table 2 reports estimates from the OLS regression of the MRW model without human capital. The specification is based on the growth approximation Equation (14), and differs from that reported in the first column of MRW's Table IV only in that the coefficients on $\log(s_i)$ and $\log(n_i + g + d)$ are constrained here to sum to zero.

Because the estimating equation is over-identified, we can derive different estimates of the rate of convergence. The method used by MRW is to invert part ii of Equation (15) to derive $\lambda = -\log(1 + \beta_1)/T$. This yields an estimated constant rate of convergence of 0.6% per year. The second method is to use the production function estimates and the observed rates of population growth to calculate the country-specific rates of convergence as $\lambda_i = (1 - \alpha)(n_i + g + d)$. This method yields country-specific rates. At the sample average rate of population growth, $n_i = 0.022$, the rate of convergence is 1.4% per year – more than twice the rate implied by the first method. This disparity

Table 1. *Descriptive statistics of MRW data for 98 non-oil countries*

	Real GDP per Worker			Annual Average	
	1960	*1985*	*Annual Growth*	*Population Growth*	*Investment/ GDP*
Average	2995	5442	1.9%	2.2%	17.7%
St. dev.	2848	5279	2.0%	0.9%	7.9%
Min.	383	412	−2.7%	0.3%	4.1%
Max.	12362	19723	10.7%	4.3%	36.9%

Source: Mankiw et al. (1992).

Table 2. *Comparing ordinary least squares and nonlinear least squares regressions of the Solow–Swan growth model*

	1	*2*	*3*
	First-order Approximation		*Exact Dynamics*
	OLS[a]	*Nonlinear Least Squares[b]*	*Nonlinear Least Squares*
Parameter estimates (t-stats)			
α	0.80 (18.5)	0.71 (33)	0.70 (31)
g	[0.02][c]	[0.02]	0.033 (3.9)
d	[0.03]	[0.03]	[0.03]
A_0	55.8 (0.97)	260 (4.5)	[160]
Summary statistics			
log-likelihood	−34.9	−50.1	−47.4
s.e. of estimate	0.35	0.40	0.39
Implied annual convergence rate			
MRW constant λ^d	0.006		
Sample average of country-specific λ_i^e	0.014	0.021	0.022

Column 1 reports estimation of Equation (14); column 2 reports estimation of Equation (13); and column 3 reports estimation of Equation (20). T-statistics are reported in round brackets.
[a] The parameter estimates in column 1 are derived from OLS regression coefficients in Equation (14) as $\alpha = \beta_2(\beta_2 - \beta_1)$ and $A_0 = \exp((0.5 - \beta_0)/\beta_1)$.
[b] The nonlinear estimation is carried out using the default maximum likelihood method in Shazam – see White (1987).
[c] Parameter values in square brackets are imposed constants.
[d] MRW calculate a constant value, $\lambda = -\log(1 + \beta_1)/25$, from Equation (14).
[e] The country-specific convergence rates are $\lambda_i = (1 - \alpha)(n_i + g + d)$. The sample average is $(1 - \alpha)(0.072)$.

gives some indication of the implications of the over-identification problem.

Neither of these methods is, however, correct since we are estimating a nonlinear model by OLS. Switching to nonlinear least squares (NLLS) estimation of the approximate growth equation (13) also avoids the problem of over-identification.

We find that the NLLS estimation procedure does not converge when we allow both d and g to be estimated freely. Accordingly, we follow MRW by assuming a 3% depreciation rate and a 2% rate of exogenous technological progress. The second column in Table 2 reports the NLLS parameters of the model, yielding an estimate of $\alpha = 0.71$, which is significantly lower than MRW's estimate of 0.80. This lower value of α implies faster convergence, averaging 2.1% per year across the 98 countries in the sample.[2]

Finally, we estimate the exact growth Equation (20). The results of the NLLS estimation are presented in column 3 of Table 2. Imposing the MRW values of 0.02 and 0.03 on g and d, the estimate for α is 0.73, which is slightly higher than the NLLS estimate for the approximate equation. The nonlinear estimation procedure does not converge if we allow free estimation of all four regression parameters, but we find that we can increase the log-likelihood ratio by imposing the previously estimated value of $A_0 = 160$ and freely estimating g. Using this two-step procedure, the estimate for α drops to 0.70, implying that the average rate of convergence is 2.2% per year.

CONCLUDING COMMENTS

Re-estimation of the MRW version of Solow–Swan transitional dynamics, using an appropriate non-linear regression technique, reveals that their misspecified linear regression causes over-estimation of the output–capital elasticity and, hence, underestimation of the rate of convergence. To the extent that subsequent empirical studies have been based on the same misspecification, many recent estimates of rates of convergence must be treated with caution.

The results presented in this chapter fail to support the first generation of endogenous growth theories which predicted unconditional divergence. Indeed, our estimates strengthen the rejection of that prediction. This does not, however, mean that more recent models of endogenous technological change are necessarily rejected. A series of papers have estimated growth models on panel data, using the time dimension as well as the cross-country dimension, to test whether the neoclassical assumption of common technology is warranted. This assumption has been strongly rejected by the results of Islam (1995) and Lee et al. (1997).

Dowrick and Rogers (2002) have estimated a model that allows for endogenous growth in domestic technology, complemented by international technology spillovers. These spillovers make an important contribution to the pattern of growth, with convergence in capital

---

[2] Carrying out equivalent tests on the human-capital augmented models, we also find that OLS understates the rate of convergence compared with NLLS estimation.

intensity and technological convergence each contributing around four percentage points to the overall rate of conditional convergence.

Adding international technology spillovers to endogenous growth models is sufficient to nullify the extreme prediction of long-run divergence across all countries. Let one component of technical progress be determined by factors specific to each country, as in models of endogenous technical progress by Romer (1990) or Aghion and Howitt (1992). Let another additive component of technical progress be due to technology transfer from the leading technology country, with the rate of transfer being a function of the technology gap. In the long run, the technological leader will be the country with the highest endogenous growth rate. Other countries, with slower endogenous growth and lower levels of technology, may benefit sufficiently from technology transfer so as to equate their long-run growth rates with the technology leader and maintain a constant long-run technology ratio. There may be some countries that fall out of the convergence club if their low rates of endogenous innovation are accompanied by an inability to exploit international spillovers, as suggested by Abramovitz (1986). The chapter by Aghion et al. (2003) in this volume (Chapter 3) comes to similar conclusions based on a model where international spillovers are industry-specific.

REFERENCES

Abramovitz, Moses (1986), "Catching Up, Forging Ahead, and Falling Behind," *Journal of Economic History* 46: 385–406.

Aghion, Philippe, Cecilia and Peter Howitt (1992), "A Model of Growth Through Creative Destruction," *Econometrica* 60(March): 323–51.

Aghion, Philippe, Cecilia García-Peñalosa, and Peter Howitt (2003), "Knowledge and Development: A Schumpeterian Approach," in Steve Dowrick, Rohan Pitchford, and Stephen J. Turnovsky (eds.), *Economic Growth and Macroeconomic Dynamics*, Cambridge University Press, Cambridge, UK, Chap. 3.

Barro, Robert J., and Xavier Sala-i-Martín (1995), *Economic Growth*, McGraw-Hill, New York, London, and Montreal.

Brander, James A., and Steve Dowrick (1994), "The Role of Fertility and Population in Economic Growth: Empirical Results from Aggregate Cross-National Data," *Journal of Population Economics* 7(1): 1–25.

Dowrick, Steve, and Mark Rogers (2002), "Classical and Technological Convergence: Beyond the Solow–Swan Growth Model," *Oxford Economic Papers* 54: 369–85.

Islam, Nazrul (1995), "Growth Empirics: A Panel Data Approach," *Quarterly Journal of Economics* 110(4): 1127–70.

Jones, Charles I. (1995), "Time Series Tests of Endogenous Growth Models," *Quarterly Journal of Economics* 110(2): 495–525.

Lee, Kevin, M. Hashem Pesaran, and Ron Smith (1997), "Growth and Convergence in a Multi-Country Empirical Stochastic Solow Model," *Journal of Applied Econometrics* 12: 357–92.

Lucas, Robert E., Jr. (1988), "On the Mechanics of Economic Development," *Journal of Monetary Economics* 22(1): 3–42.

Mankiw, N. Gregory, David Romer, and David N. Weil (1992), "A Contribution to the Empirics of Economic Growth," *Quarterly Journal of Economics* 107(2): 407–37.

Romer, Paul M. (1990), "Endogenous Technological Change," *Journal of Political Economy* 98(5): S1971–1102.

White, K. J. (1987), "A General Computer Program for Econometric Methods – Shazam," *Econometrica* January: 239–40.

5

Bifurcations in Macroeconomic Models

William A. Barnett and Yijun He

1. INTRODUCTION

Modern macroeconomics has witnessed the increasing use of dynamic models in the study of economic behavior. Among the widely recognized models are the Bergstrom and Wymer continuous time dynamic macroeconometric model of the UK economy (Bergstrom and Wymer, 1976), the Leeper and Sims (1994) model, and the dynamic Leontief systems (Luenberger and Arbel, 1977).

Grandmont (1985) found that the parameter space of even the simplest, most classical models is stratified into bifurcation regions. But in such classical models all policies are Ricardian equivalent and all solutions are Pareto optimal. As a result he was not able to reach conclusions about policy relevance of his dramatic discovery. Barnett and He (1999, 2002) subsequently found transcritical, codimension two, and Hopf bifurcation boundaries within the parameter space of the policy-relevant Bergstrom and Wymer continuous time dynamic macroeconometric model of the UK economy.

Because of the Lucas critique, there is increasing interest in Euler equation models with generalized method of moments estimated deep parameters. He and Barnett's (2003) analysis of the Leeper and Sims (1994) Euler equations macroeconometric model revealed the existence of singularity-induced bifurcation within the model's parameter space. Although known in engineering, singularity-induced bifurcations have not previously been encountered in economics.

Euler equation models represent an important class of economic systems. In addition to the Leeper and Sims model, there is also, for example, the well-known Luenberger (Luenberger and Arbel, 1977) fundamental dynamic Leontief model. Knowledge of the nature of

singularity-induced bifurcations is likely to become increasingly important in understanding the dynamics of modern macroeconomic models.
Bifurcation analysis of parameter space stratification is a fundamental and frequently overlooked part of understanding model properties
and can provide surprising results, as we have repeatedly found.

The purpose of the chapter is to introduce the bifurcation phenomena that we have encountered in the analysis of macroeconometric
models. We include and emphasize the concept of singularity-induced
bifurcation and its relationship to other forms of bifurcation. We do so
for the benefit of economists who might encounter singularity bifurcation in the future, as we believe to be likely with other Euler equation
models similarly parameterized with deep parameters. The theory of
singularity-induced bifurcation is still in the process of developing.
Therefore, we use examples to illustrate the effect of the presence of
this type of bifurcation on system behaviors.

2. STABILITY

Many existing dynamic macroeconomic models can be written in the
following general form:

$$\mathbf{Dx} = \mathbf{f}(\mathbf{x}, \theta), \tag{1}$$

where $\mathbf{D}$ is the differentiation operator, $\mathbf{x}$ is the state vector, θ is the
parameter vector, and $\mathbf{f}$ is the vector of functions that governs the
dynamics of the system. Every component of $\mathbf{f}(\mathbf{x}, \theta)$ is smooth (infinitely
continuously differentiable) in a local region of interest. For example,
the well-known Bergstrom continuous time UK macroeconomic model
can be written in the form (1) (Barnett and He, 1999). In the language
of systems theory, system (1) is the class of first-order autonomous
systems.

For system (1), there may exist a point $\mathbf{x}^*$ such that $\mathbf{f}(\mathbf{x}^*, \theta) = \mathbf{0}$.
Then $\mathbf{x}^*$ is an equilibrium. When started at x^*, the system will stay
there forever. Without loss of generality, we may assume that $\mathbf{x}^* = \mathbf{0}$
(by replacing x with $x - x^*$).

The value of the parameter vector θ can affect the dynamics of system
(1). Let us assume that θ can take values within a possible set Θ. It can
be important to now how the value of the parameter vector can change
the behavior of system (1).

One basic property of a system is its stability. If $\mathbf{x}^*$ is an equilibrium of system (1), we know that system (1) stays at $\mathbf{x}^*$ forever if the system starts at equilibrium. One would also like to know what would happen if the system starts not exactly at $\mathbf{x}^*$ but in a neighborhood of it. Stability answers that question and related questions.

We now introduce theory regarding stability of a system such as system (1) around the equilibrium $\mathbf{x}^* = \mathbf{0}$. For this purpose, let us rewrite system (1) as

$$\mathbf{Dx} = A(\theta)\mathbf{x} + \mathbf{F}(\mathbf{x}, \theta), \tag{2}$$

where $A(\theta)$ is the Jacobian matrix of $\mathbf{f}(\mathbf{x}, \theta)$ acquired by differentiating $\mathbf{f}$ with respect to $\mathbf{x}$ and evaluating the resulting matrix at the equilibrium $\mathbf{x}^* = \mathbf{0}$. The matrix $A(\theta)$ is the coefficient matrix of the linear terms, and

$$\mathbf{F}(\mathbf{x}, \theta) = \mathbf{f}(\mathbf{x}, \theta) - A(\theta)\mathbf{x} = o(\mathbf{x})$$

is the vector of higher order terms. In nonlinear systems theory, the local stability of system (1) can be studied by examining the eigenvalues of the coefficient matrix $A(\theta)$, as follows:

(a) If all eigenvalues of $A(\theta)$ have strictly negative real parts, then system (1) is locally asymptotically stable in the neighborhood of $\mathbf{x} = \mathbf{0}$.

(b) If at least one of the eigenvalues of $A(\theta)$ has positive real part, then system (1) is locally asymptotically unstable in the neighborhood of $\mathbf{x} = \mathbf{0}$.

(c) If all eigenvalues of $A(\theta)$ have nonpositive real parts and at least one has zero real part, the stability of system (1) usually cannot be determined from the matrix $A(\theta)$. One needs to analyze higher order terms in order to determine the stability of the system. In most cases, one needs to examine the system behavior along a certain manifold to determine the stability.

Because $A(\theta)$ is a function of the parameter vector θ, the stability of system (1) could be dependent on θ. Consequently, it is important to know for what parameter values system (1) is stable and for what values it is not. It is also important to know the nature of the instability, and when the system unstable.

The values of θ such that system (1) is stable define a stable region S of the parameter space. In order to determine S, we need to find its boundaries. We now examine how to determine the boundary of the stability region. According to conditions (a)–(c), the boundary could only happen under condition (c), so $A(\theta)$ has at least one zero eigenvalue. On the boundary, we also need to determine the stability of the system, but finding the boundary provides the crucial step.

We know from matrix theory that $A(\theta)$ has at least one zero eigenvalue if and only if

$$\det(A(\theta)) = 0. \tag{3}$$

In principle, Equation (3) identifies the stability boundary. But when θ is multi-dimensional, it can be difficult to solve for the values of θ that satisfy Equation (3). In some cases, it is possible to reduce Equation (3) into a solvable form such that a closed-form solution can be obtained. Otherwise, it might be possible to solve Equation (3) numerically. Some interesting cases were reported by Barnett and He (1999, 2002), in which we apply various methods to solve and display stability boundaries characterized by Equation (3).

We need to introduce a concept that is important in identifying boundary points. An equilibrium point $\mathbf{x}^*$ of system (1) is called *hyperbolic* if the coefficient matrix $A(\theta)$ has no eigenvalues with zero real parts. For a hyperbolic equilibrium $\mathbf{x}^*$, the asymptotic behavior of system (1) is determined by the eigenvalues of $A(\theta)$ according to conditions (a) and (b). The behavior of nonhyperbolic equilibria can be especially interesting.

3. BIFURCATIONS IN MACROECONOMICS

One way of studying system properties, when the values of the system's parameters are not known with certainty, is through bifurcation analysis. Bifurcation refers to a class of phenomena in dynamic systems such that the dynamic properties of the system change when parameters cross a boundary. When the location of a system's parameters is not known with certainty, it is important to know about the existence and location of such bifurcation boundaries and to explore on which side of the boundaries the parameters lie. Bifurcation boundaries have been discovered in many macroeconomic systems. The types of bifurcation boundaries found include Hopf bifurcations in growth models (e.g., Benhabib and Nishimura, 1979; Boldrin and Woodford, 1990; Dockner and Feichtinger, 1991; Nishimura and Takahashi, 1992), pitchfork bifurcations in the tatonnement process (e.g., Bala, 1997; Scarf, 1960), and transcritical bifurcations (Barnett and He, 1999). Bifurcations are especially interesting with regard to dynamic macroeconomic systems, since several well-known models, including Bergstrom and Wymer's (1976) UK model, operate close to bifurcation boundaries between stable and unstable regions of the parameter space.

For small perturbations of parameters, there are no structural changes in the dynamics of a hyperbolic equilibrium, provided the perturbations are sufficiently small. Therefore, bifurcations can occur only in the local neighborhood of nonhyperbolic equilibria.

3.1. Transcritical Bifurcations

A transcritical bifurcation occurs when a system has a non-hyperbolic equilibrium with a geometrically simple zero eigenvalue at the bifurcation point, and when additional transversality conditions also are satisfied [given by Sotomayor's theorem (1973)].

For a one-dimensional system,

$$Dx = G(x, \theta),$$

the transversality conditions for a transcritical bifurcation at $(x, \theta) = (0, 0)$ are

$$G(0, 0) = G_x(0, 0) = 0, \quad G_\theta(0, 0) = 0, \quad G_{xx}(0, 0) \neq 0, \quad \text{and}$$
$$G_{\theta x}^2 - G_{xx}G_{\theta\theta}(0, 0) > 0. \tag{4}$$

The canonical form of such systems is

$$Dx = \theta x - x^2. \tag{5}$$

Note that Equation (5) is stable around the equilibrium $x^* = 0$ for $\theta < 0$ and unstable for $\theta > 0$. The equilibrium $x^* = \theta$ is stable for $\theta > 0$ and unstable for $\theta < 0$.

Figure 1 illustrates the resulting transcritical bifurcation. In Figure 1, the solid line represents stable equilibrium points, whereas the dashed line shows unstable ones.

Transcritical bifurcations have been found in high-dimensional continuous-time macroeconometric systems. In high-dimensional cases, transversality conditions have to be verified on a certain manifold. See Guckenheimer and Holmes (1983) for details.

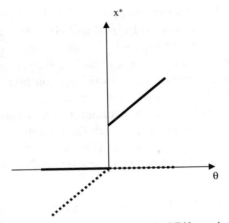

Figure 1. Diagram of Transcritical Bifurcation.

3.2. Pitchfork Bifurcations

The standard one-dimensional system with a pitchfork bifurcation is

$$Dx = \theta x - x^3.$$

For each $\theta > 0$, this system has three equilibria: $x^* = 0$ (unstable), and $\pm\sqrt{\theta}$ (stable). For every $\theta < 0$, there is only one (stable) equilibrium $x^* = 0$. Figure 2 is its bifurcation diagram.

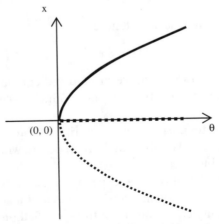

Figure 2. Diagram of Pitchfork Bifurcation.

Transversality conditions can be obtained as follows. Consider a one-variable, one-parameter differential equation

$$Dx = f(x, \theta).$$

Suppose that there exists an equilibrium x^* and a parameter value θ^* such that (x^*, θ^*) satisfies the following conditions:

(a) $\dfrac{\partial f(x, \theta^*)}{\partial x}\big|_{x=x^*} = 0,$

(b) $\dfrac{\partial^3 f(x, \theta^*)}{\partial x^3}\big|_{x=x^*} \neq 0,$

(c) $\dfrac{\partial^2 f(x, \theta)}{\partial x \partial \theta}\big|_{x=x^*, \theta=\theta^*} \neq 0.$

Then (x^*, θ^*) is a pitchfork bifurcation point. Depending on the signs of the transversality conditions, the equilibrium x^* could change from stable to unstable when the parameter θ crosses θ^*.

Consider the differential equation

$$Dx = \theta x - x^3.$$

We find that $x^* = 0$ and $x^* = \pm\sqrt{\theta}$ are equilibria. The Jacobian is $\theta - 3x^2$, which is equal to zero when $x = 0$ and $\theta = 0$. The transversality conditions are also satisfied at $(0, 0)$. Hence, the point $(0, 0)$ is a pitchfork bifurcation point. Judging by the sign of $\theta - 3x^2$, we can see that the equilibrium $x^* = 0$ is stable when $\theta < 0$ and unstable when $\theta > 0$. The two other equilibria $x^* = \pm\sqrt{\theta}$ are stable for $\theta > 0$. In this case, pitchfork bifurcation is said to be supercritical. Otherwise, the pitchfork bifurcation is subcritical.

Bala (1997) explains how pitchfork bifurcation occurs in the tatonnement process. Consider an economy consisting of two goods and two agents. The process consists of two goods and two agents. The agents have constant elasticity of substitution utility functions parameterized by $\mu \in [0, 1]$. The utility functions and endowments of agents 1 and 2 are

$$\mu^1(x_1, x_2, \mu) = -x_1^{\mu/(\mu-1)} - 2^{1/(\mu-1)}x_2^{\mu/(\mu-1)}$$

$$\mu^2(x_1, x_2, \mu) = -2^{1/(\mu-1)}x_1^{\mu/(\mu-1)} - x_2^{\mu/(\mu-1)},$$

where x_1 and x_2 are the amounts of the two goods that are consumed. Let the price of good 2 be normalized to be 1, and let p denote the price of good 1. The following are the resultant excess demand functions for the economy e_μ:

$$z_1(p, \mu) = \frac{2p^\mu}{2p^\mu + 1} + \frac{p^{\mu-1}}{p^\mu + 2} - 1$$

$$z_2(p, \mu) = \frac{p}{2p^\mu + 1} + \frac{2}{p^\mu + 2} - 1.$$

The tatonnement process for the economy e_μ is given by

$$Dp = z_1(p, \mu).$$

Bala (1997) shows that pitchfork bifurcation exists in this system and, furthermore, that for any $\mu \in (3/4, 1)$, the economy e_μ has three equilibria. Chaos also exists in the tatonnement process, as shown by Bala and Majumdar (1992).

3.3. Saddle-Node Bifurcations

The standard system with a pitchfork bifurcation is

$$Dx = \theta - x^2.$$

Note that it differs from the basic system for transcritical bifurcation by replacing the first-order term with the zero-order parameter and from the basic system for pitchfork bifurcation by lowering the orders of both terms. There exists no equilibrium for $\theta < 0$. For any given $\theta > 0$, this system has two equilibria, $x^* = \pm\sqrt{\theta}$. Figure 3 shows the bifurcation diagram.

Saddle-node bifurcation is generic in the sense that a general system in which $A(\theta)$ has a simple zero eigenvalue displays a saddle-node bifurcation under small perturbations.

For a general one-dimensional system,

$$Dx = f(x, \theta).$$

Let x^* be a non-hyperbolic equilibrium, and let θ^* be the corresponding parameter, so that (x^*, θ^*) satisfies

$$\frac{\partial f(x, \theta^*)}{\partial x}\Big|_{x=x^*} = 0,$$

$$f(x^*, \theta^*) = 0.$$

Then the transversality conditions for saddle-node bifurcations are

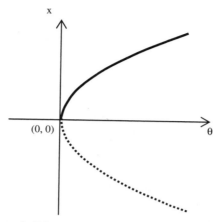

Figure 3. Diagram for Saddle-Node Bifurcation.

$$\text{(a)} \ \frac{\partial f(x, \theta)}{\partial \theta}\Big|_{x=x^*, \theta=\theta^*} \neq 0,$$

$$\text{(b)} \ \frac{\partial^2 f(x, \theta)}{\partial x^2}\Big|_{x=x^*, \theta=\theta^*} \neq 0.$$

Transversality conditions for high-dimensional systems can also be formulated (see Sotomayor, 1973).

The following economic system (Gandolfo, 1996) exhibits saddle-node bifurcation:

$$Dr = v[F(r, \alpha) - S(r)],$$

where r is the spot exchange rate defined as domestic currency per foreign currency, $v > 0$ is the adjustment speed, α is a parameter, and $\partial F / \partial \alpha > 0$. The differential equation indicates that the exchange rate adjusts according to the excess demand. In deriving the model, it is assumed that the demand for and supply of foreign exchange come solely from traders and that the supply curve is backward-bending (which is viewed to be normal). Therefore, there could exist two points of intersection between the demand curve and the supply curve as well as one point of tangency between the two curves. For this system, it can be verified that the transversality conditions for saddle-node bifurcations are satisfied. Hence, the tangent point (r^*, α^*) is a saddle-node bifurcation.

3.4. Hopf Bifurcations

Hopf bifurcations are probably the most studied type of bifurcations. Such bifurcations occur at points at which the system has a non-hyperbolic equilibrium with a pair of purely imaginary eigenvalues, but without zero eigenvalues. Also, additional transversality conditions must be satisfied (see the Hopf Theorem in Guckenheimer and Holmes, 1983).

Hopf bifurcation requires the presence of a pair of purely imaginary eigenvalues; hence, the dimension of a system needs to be at least 2. The transversality conditions, which are rather lengthy, are given by Glendinning (1994). The basic requirements are (1) the occurrence of a pair of purely imaginary eigenvalues and (2) that the system crosses the stability boundary with nonzero zero. The canonical form of such systems is

$$Dx = -y + x(\theta - (x^2 + y^2)),$$
$$Dy = x + y(\theta - (x^2 + y^2)).$$

It has a pair of conjugate eigenvalues $\theta + i$ and $\theta - i$. The eigenvalues are purely imaginary when $\theta = 0$, which is the bifurcation point.

The Hopf bifurcation boundaries could be determined numerically. Consider the case of $\det(A(\theta)) \neq 0$, when $A(\theta)$ has at least one pair of purely imaginary eigenvalues. If $A(\theta)$ has exactly one such pair, and if some additional transversality conditions hold, this point is on a Hopf bifurcation boundary.

To find Hopf bifurcation points, let $p(s) = \det(sI - A)$ be the characteristic polynomial of A, and express it as

$$p(s) = c_0 + c_1 s + c_2 s^2 + c_3 s^3 + \cdots + c_{n-1} s^{n-1} + s^n.$$

Construct the following $(n-1) \times (n-1)$ matrix:

$$S = \begin{bmatrix} c_0 & c_2 & \cdots & c_{n-2} & 1 & 0 & 0 & \cdots & 0 \\ 0 & c_0 & c_2 & \cdots & c_{n-2} & 1 & 0 & \cdots & 0 \\ & & \cdots & & & & & & \\ 0 & 0 & \cdots & 0 & c_0 & c_2 & c_4 & \cdots & 1 \\ c_1 & c_3 & \cdots & c_{n-1} & 0 & 0 & 0 & \cdots & 0 \\ 0 & c_1 & c_3 & \cdots & c_{n-1} & 0 & 0 & \cdots & 0 \\ & & \cdots & & & & & & \\ 0 & 0 & \cdots & 0 & c_1 & c_3 & \cdots & \cdots & c_{n-1} \end{bmatrix}.$$

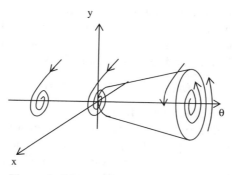

Figure 4. Diagram for Hopf Bifurcation.

Let S_0 be obtained by deleting rows 1 and $n/2$ and columns 1 and 2, and let S_1 be obtained by deleting rows 1 and $n/2$ and columns 1 and 3. Then the matrix $A(\theta)$ has exactly one pair of purely imaginary eigenvalues (see, e.g., Guckenheimer et al., 1997) if

$$\det(S) = 0, \qquad \det(S_0)\det(S_1) > 0. \qquad (6)$$

If $\det(S) \neq 0$ or if $\det(S_0)\det(S_1) < 0$, then $A(\theta)$ has no purely imaginary eigenvalues. If $\det(S) = 0$ and $\det(S_0)\det(S_1) = 0$, then $A(\theta)$ may have more than one pair of purely imaginary eigenvalues. Therefore, the second condition for a bifurcation boundary is

$$\det(S) = 0, \qquad \det(S_0)\det(S_1) \neq 0. \qquad (7)$$

Condition (7) could be used to find candidates for bifurcation boundaries, and then the candidate segments could be checked to determine which are true boundaries. Since solving Condition (7) analytically is impossible with realistic cases, a numerical procedure was provided by Barnett and He (1999) to find bifurcation boundaries. The stability of Condition (7) at parameter values on the bifurcation boundary can be analyzed in the same manner as for transcritical bifurcations. Figure 4 shows the bifurcation diagram for Hopf bifurcations.

4. SINGULARITY-INDUCED BIFURCATIONS

In Section 3, we reviewed some well-documented bifurcation regions encountered in macroeconomic models. We devote this section to a recently discovered surprising bifurcation region found in the Leeper and Sims (1994) bifurcation model: singularity-induced bifurcation.

Some macroeconomic models, such as the widely recognized dynamic Leontief model and the Leeper and Sims model, have the form

$$E\mathbf{x}(n+1) = A\mathbf{x}(n) + \mathbf{f}(n), \tag{8}$$

in which $\mathbf{x}(n)$ is the state vector, $\mathbf{f}(n)$ is the vector of driving variables, n is time, and E and A are constant matrices of appropriate dimensions. The most significant aspect of Equation (8) is the possibility that the matrix E could be singular. If E is always invertible, then Equation (8) will be in the discrete-time form of Equation (1).

Model (8) in continuous time has the following form:

$$E(\mathbf{x}, \boldsymbol{\theta})D\mathbf{x} = \mathbf{F}(\mathbf{x}, \boldsymbol{\theta}). \tag{9}$$

Singularity-induced bifurcation occurs when the rank of $E(\mathbf{x}, \boldsymbol{\theta})$ changes, such as from an invertible matrix to a singular one. In such cases, the dimension of the dynamic part of the system changes accordingly. To see this point, for any given form of Equation (9), we can always perform appropriate coordinate transformation so that Equation (9) is equivalent to the following form:

$$E_1(\mathbf{x}_1, \mathbf{x}_2, \boldsymbol{\theta})D\mathbf{x}_1 = \mathbf{F}_1(\mathbf{x}_1, \mathbf{x}_2, \boldsymbol{\theta})$$
$$\mathbf{0} = \mathbf{F}_2(\mathbf{x}_1, \mathbf{x}_2, \boldsymbol{\theta}).$$

For this reason, System (9) is often referred to as a differential-algebraic system.

The structural properties of the dynamics for Equation (9) are substantially more complex than those for Equation (1). Standard forms are available in bifurcation analysis of Equation (1), but no canonical forms are available for Equation (9). When $E = I$, Equation (9) becomes Equation (1). In that case bifurcations can be classified according to the canonical forms obtained from transforming A. The values that E may take create a large number of possibilities.

We use the following examples to demonstrate the complexity of bifurcation behavior of Equation (9).

Example 5.1: Consider the following system modified from the canonical system for transcritical bifurcation:

$$D x = \theta x - x^2 \tag{10}$$

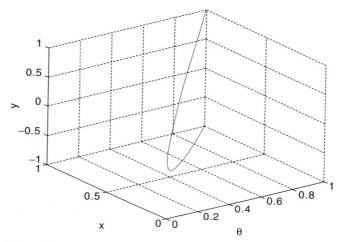

Figure 5. Bifurcation Diagram for System (10)–(11) for $\theta > 0$.

$$0 = x - y^2. \tag{11}$$

The equilibria now become $(0, 0)$ and $(\theta, \pm\sqrt{\theta})$. In this case, System (10)–(11) is stable around the equilibrium $(x^*, y^*) = (0, 0)$ for $\theta < 0$ and unstable for $\theta > 0$. The equilibrium $(x^*, y^*) = (0, \pm\sqrt{\theta})$ is undefined when $\theta < 0$ and unstable when $\theta > 0$. Figure 5 shows the three-dimensional bifurcation diagram for this system.

Example 5.2: The following system is modified from the canonical system for saddle-point bifurcation:

$$Dx = \theta - x^2 \tag{12}$$
$$0 = x - y^2. \tag{13}$$

The equilibria are $(\sqrt{\theta}, \pm\sqrt[4]{\theta})$, which are defined only for $\theta > 0$. In this case, System (12)–(13) is stable around both equilibria. Figure 6 shows the three-dimensional bifurcation diagram for this system.

The form of matrix E is fixed to be

$$E = \begin{bmatrix} 1 & 0 \\ 0 & 0 \end{bmatrix}$$

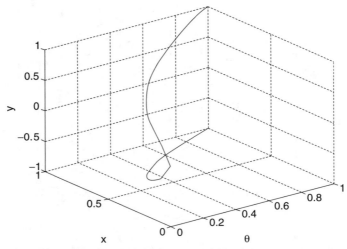

Figure 6. Bifurcation Diagram for System (12)–(13).

in both Examples 5.1 and 5.2. However, in some systems, such as the Leeper and Sims model, the matrix E is also parameterized. The following example demonstrates bifurcation in such cases.

Example 5.3: Consider the system

$$Dx = ax - x^2 \tag{14}$$
$$\theta Dy = x - y^2, \tag{15}$$

in which $a > 0$. For every θ, the equilibria are $(0, 0)$ and $(a, \pm\sqrt{a})$. In this case, System (14)–(15) is unstable around the equilibrium $(x^*, y^*) = (0, 0)$ for any value of θ. The equilibrium $(x^*, y^*) = (a, +\sqrt{a})$ is unstable for $\theta < 0$ and stable for $\theta > 0$, although the value of the equilibrium does not depend on θ at all. The third equilibrium $(x^*, y^*) = (a, -\sqrt{a})$ is unstable for $\theta > 0$ and stable for $\theta < 0$.

The effect of adding the second dynamic equation is more visible if we consider the System (14)–(15) in phase plan.

Figure 7 clearly shows the stability of the equilibrium point $(1, 1)$ and the instability of $(1, -1)$ and $(0, 0)$. It displays two-dimensional dynamics for any $\theta \neq 0$. However, when $\theta = 0$, the system behavior degenerates into the movement along the curve $x - y^2 = 0$, as shown in Figure 8.

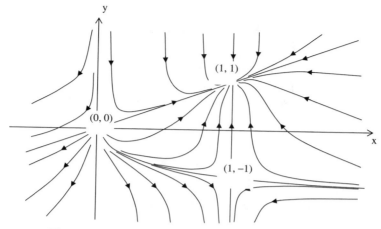

Figure 7. Phase Portrait of System (14)–(15) for $\theta > 0$.

Example 5.4: If the second equation in System (14)–(15) is changed to be linear, such that

$$Dx = ax - x^2 \qquad (16)$$
$$\theta Dy = x - y, \qquad (17)$$

then for every θ the equilibria are $(0, 0)$ and (a, a). In this case, system (15)–(16) is unstable around the equilibrium $(x^*, y^*) = (0, 0)$ for any value of θ. The equilibrium $(x^*, y^*) = (a, a)$ is unstable for $\theta < 0$ and stable for $\theta > 0$. Again the value of the equilibrium does not depend on θ at all. Figures 9 and 10 show the phase portraits for system (16)–(17) for $\theta > 0$ and for $\theta = 0$, respectively.

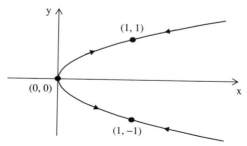

Figure 8. Phase Portrait of System (14)–(15) for $\theta = 0$.

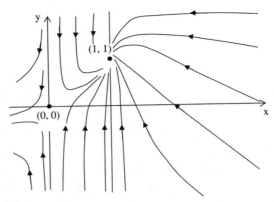

Figure 9. Phase Portrait of System (16)–(17) for $\theta > 0$.

Again, Figures 9 and 10 demonstrate the drastic changes of dynamical properties that occur when the parameter traverses the bifurcation boundary. When $\theta = 0$, the variable y in System (16)–(17) is just a replica of the variable x in system (16)–(17). The real independent dynamics is just one-dimensional. However, when $\theta \neq 0$, the system moves into a two-dimensional space. The variable y follows x with some deviation error. The error asymptotically diminishes to zero.

Changes in the dynamical properties of Equation (9) can reflect more than a simple change of the rank of E. In fact, even with the same rank of E, the order of the dynamical part of Equation (9) could still vary

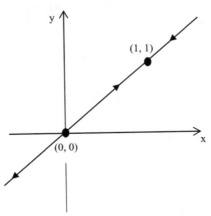

Figure 10. Phase Portrait of System (16)–(17) for $\theta = 0$.

when parameters take different values, as illustrated in the following example.

Example 5.5: Consider the following system:

$$Dx_1 = x_3$$
$$Dx_2 = -x_2$$
$$0 = x_1 + x_2 + \theta x_3. \tag{18}$$

For any $\theta \neq 0$, solving from the last equation results in

$$Dx_1 = -(x_1 + x_2)/\theta$$
$$Dx_2 = -x_2, \tag{19}$$

which is stable at the equilibrium $(0, 0)$ for $\theta > 0$ and unstable at equilibrium $(0, 0)$ for $\theta < 0$.

Solving from the last of Equations (18) when $\theta = 0$, we obtain

$$x_1 = -x_2$$
$$x_3 = x_2$$
$$Dx_2 = -x_2 \tag{20}$$

for any $t > 0$. Note the difference of the order of dynamics in Equations (20) from that of Equations (19)!

5. CONCLUSION

In this chapter, we have provided a summary of some well-documented bifurcation phenomena in macroeconomic models. Most notably, we have introduced singularity-induced bifurcations, which have not previously been encountered in economics and which He and Barnett (2003) surprisingly recently discovered in the Leeper and Sims Euler equations macroeconometric model. Although many interesting results have been obtained in the existing literature, bifurcation theory in economic dynamics is far from complete.

REFERENCES

Bala, V. (1997), "A Pitchfork Bifurcation in the Tatonnement Process," *Economic Theory* 10: 521–30.

Bala, V., and M. Majumdar (1992), "Chaotic Tatonnement," *Economic Theory* 2: 437–45.

Barnett, William A., and Yijun He (1999), "Stability Analysis of Continuous-Time Macroeconometric Systems," *Studies in Nonlinear Dynamics and Econometrics* 3(4): 169–88.

Barnett, William A., and Yijun He (2002), "Stabilization Policy as Bifurcation Selection: Would Stabilization Policy Work If the Economy Really Were Unstable?" *Macroeconomic Dynamics* 6(5): 713–47.

Benhabib, J., and K. Nishimura (1979), "The Hopf Bifurcation and the Existence and Stability of Closed Orbits in Multisector Models of Optimal Economic Growth," *Journal of Economic Theory* 21: 421–44.

Bergstrom, A. R., and C. R. Wymer (1976), "A Model of Disequilibrium Neoclassic Growth and Its Application to the United Kingdom," in A. R. Bergstrom (ed.), *Statistical Inference in Continuous Time Economic Models*, North Holland, Amsterdam, pp. 267–327.

Boldrin, M., and M. Woodford (1990), "Equilibrium Models Displaying Endogenous Fluctuations and Chaos: A Survey," *Journal of Monetary Economics* 25: 189–222.

Dockner, E. J., and G. Feichtinger (1991), "On the Optimality of Limit Cycles in Dynamic Economic Systems," *Journal of Economics* 51: 31–50.

Gandolfo, G. (1996), *Economic Dynamics*, Springer, New York.

Glendinning, P. (1994), *Stability, Instability, and Chaos*, Cambridge University Press, Cambridge, UK.

Grandmont, J. M. (1985), "On Endogenous Competitive Business Cycles," *Econometrica* 53: 995–1045.

Guckenheimer, J., and P. Holmes (1983), *Nonlinear Oscillations, Dynamical Systems, and Bifurcations of Vector Fields*, Springer-Verlag, New York.

Guckenheimer, J., M. Myers, and B. Sturmfels (1997), "Computing Hopf Bifurcations I," *SIAM Journal of Numerical Analysis* 34: 1–21.

He, Yijun, and William A. Barnett (2003), "New Phenomena Identified in a Stochastic Dynamic Macroeconometric Model: A Bifurcation Perspective," *Journal of Econometrics*, forthcoming.

Leeper, E., and C. Sims (1994), "Toward a Modern Macro Model Usable for Policy Analysis," in *NBER Macroeconomics Annual*, National Bureau of Economic Research, New York, pp. 81–117.

Luenberger, D. G., and A. Arbel (1977), "Singular Dynamic Leontief Systems," *Econometrica* 45: 991–96.

Nishimura, K., and H. Takahashi (1992), "Factor Intensity and Hopf Bifurcations," in G. Feichtinger (ed.), *Dynamic Economic Models and Optimal Control*, North Holland, Amsterdam, pp. 135–49.

Scarf, H. (1960), "Some Examples of Global Instability of Competitive Equilibrium," *International Economic Review* 1(3): 157–72.

Sotomayor, J. (1973), "Generic Bifurcations of Dynamic Systems," in M. M. Peixoto (ed.), *Dynamical Systems*, Academic Press, New York, pp. 561–82.

PART THREE

Dynamic Issues in International Economics

6

Dynamic Trade Creation

Eric O'N. Fisher and Neil Vousden

1. INTRODUCTION

The emergence of large trading blocs as a central feature of the world economy has led to renewed interest in customs unions and free trade areas. Analysis of preferential trading arrangements has traditionally focused on static trade creation and diversion. However, as world capital markets have become increasingly integrated, it is clear that the *dynamic* effects of trade policy are also of great significance.

The analysis of preferential trading areas necessarily involves changes from a tariff-ridden equilibrium, so we are already in a world of the second best. Hence, it would not help further to muddy the analytical waters by assuming that the source of growth is some economy-wide externality. Thus we are drawn to the class of growth models studied by Jones and Manuelli (1990) and Rebelo (1991). Also, because we are interested in the effects of commercial policies across time, it is natural to assume that agents do not live forever. Thus, we maintain analytical simplicity by imposing the discipline of a strictly neoclassical framework with no increasing returns and no bequest motives.

The burden of this discipline is that endogenous economic growth can occur only if the economy has at least two sectors.[1] The most natural economy has a consumption sector, an investment sector, a

---

[1] Thus, we hark back to an older tradition of two-sector models in international economics, originating with Uzawa (1964) and Srinivasan's (1964) extensions of Ramsey's (1928) classic. Galor (1992) has put some new wine into that old bottle.

Fisher would like to thank The Australian National University, whose hospitality made this collaboration possible. He thanks two anonymous referees, Carsten Kowalczyk, Wolfgang Mayer, and seminar participants at numerous universities and conferences for their comments on earlier drafts of this work. Neil Vousden died in Canberra on 7 December 2000; he was a fine scholar and a good man. He will be missed by all who knew him.

reproducible factor, and a fixed factor. Boldrin (1992) and Jones and Manuelli (1992) show implicitly that one-sector growth models ignore a crucial element in the development process: that investment goods become cheaper over time so that the fixed factor can afford an increasingly large stock of the reproducible factor from a finite stream of revenues. Fisher (1992) showed that the supply side of Rebelo's (1991) model captures the asymptotic behavior of a wide class of neoclassical economies where agents have finite lives and long-run growth can occur.

Why are two sectors necessary? The assumption of finite lives (without a bequest motive or an explicit role for government policy) imposes a very stark financing constraint on a growing economy. In particular, each generation must purchase an increasingly large stock of reproducible resources (capital, broadly defined) from a finite stream of revenues (lifetime labor income). Even though real wages become unboundedly large in a growing economy, the *rate of growth* of real wages does not keep up with the rate of growth of the capital stock. Thus, the financing constraint will bind eventually, and sustained growth will be impossible.

A one-sector growth model with a Cobb–Douglas production function provides some sharp intuition. In this case, endogenous growth can occur only if capital's share is unity, but then labor's share is zero. Hence, there is no source of savings from wage income, and the economy with overlapping generations cannot grow.

How can one overcome this financing constraint? There are three possibilities. First, one can assume that there is an economy-wide growth externality; indeed, this is the path that much of the modern literature has followed. For us, this tack has an unfortunate and ineluctable side effect: it introduces a further complication into a second-best world where preferential trading arrangements are already distorting. Second, one can assume that there is a role for government; permanently redistributive policies, typically in the guise of capital taxation, will overcome the financing constraint. This assumption may be tenable for the closed economy, but it is hard to see a simple analog for the open economy. Taxing domestic capital to enhance world growth typically would not be politically feasible. Third, one can assume that there are two sectors in the economy. This assumption introduces one relative price – the current price of investment (in terms of consumption forgone). Then growth can occur because the real price of investment may become increasingly cheap as the world economy develops.

Again, the Cobb–Douglas case gives sharp intuition. Consider now an economy with Cobb–Douglas production functions in two sectors. Assume that the share of labor income in the consumption sector is strictly greater than zero, and its share in the investment sector is exactly zero. The latter assumption allows the economy to grow, and the former assures that there will be some wage income in every generation. On a balanced growth path, the value shares of the two sectors in gross domestic product (GDP) remain constant. However, at constant base-year prices, the consumption sector grows more slowly than the investment-goods sector, the engine of growth for the economy. The key insight is that the GDP shares of consumption and investment remain constant only because the relative price of investment good decreases as the economy grows. Hence, the real wage can grow sufficiently rapidly to purchase a rapidly growing stock of capital from a finite stream of wage income.

Several economists have already sought to adumbrate a theoretical basis for the dynamic effects of liberalized trade. Baldwin (1992) defines and calibrates dynamic gains from trade in Europe due to induced capital accumulation along the transition between steady states in a variant of a Solow growth model. Using endogenous growth models, several authors have identified links between economic integration and growth. Some are based on externalities associated with learning by doing (e.g., Lucas, 1988; Young, 1991), and others focus on economies where novel ideas or products generate growth (e.g., Grossman and Helpman, 1991; Rivera-Batiz and Romer, 1991). Applying a hybrid of these models, Kehoe (1994) shows that Spain grew rapidly following her entry into the European Community.[2] Since the role of preferential trading regimes motivates much of this recent work, it seems appropriate to analyze these arrangements explicitly.

Our model may seem old fashioned to a modern reader. In particular, world growth occurs only because of capital accumulation. There are no economy-wide externalities, there is no emphasis on Schumpeterian innovation, and there are no simple Pareto-improving government

---

[2] Spain entered the Community in 1986. Kehoe documents a change in its trend of investment from an annual 1% decline in the five years preceding entry into an average increase of 10% per annum for the five following years. Similarly, the growth rate of foreign investment in Spain increased fivefold between those periods.

policies. These facts may cause some readers to dismiss this analysis out of hand, but we beg for a moment's indulgence. Because the analysis of preferential trading areas is already complicated enough, we are really proposing the simplest economy in which endogenous growth is possible and agents have finite lives.

The skeptical reader might further ask, why bother with overlapping generations? Isn't the standard model in macroeconomics the one with infinitely lived agents? Some might argue, quite to the contrary, that many interesting issues in general equilibrium theory arise precisely in models in which agents' lives are finite. In a model of economic growth, this has two very important implications. First, commercial policies influence both people alive now and those not yet born. In international economics, the former are Stolper–Samuelson effects, and the latter are growth-enhancing effects. Second, world growth trajectories typically cannot be Pareto ranked. In particular, increasing the rate of world growth is usually *not* Pareto improving.

In international economics, this observation gives rise to an important subtlety in the analysis of any commercial policy. There are four classes of agents that matter: (1) the current generation at home, (2) their counter-parts abroad, (3) future generations at home, and (4) their counter-parts abroad. Consider, for example, a domestic tariff that protects a capital-intensive industry in a two-by-two economy. The Stolper–Samuelson effects imply a rise in the real income of domestic capitalists and a fall in that of domestic workers. If the tariff reduces domestic imports of capital-intensive goods, it will also lower the real income of foreign capitalists and raise the real income of laborers abroad. The effect that such a tariff has on the world growth trajectory is also obviously important, and it will surely influence an infinite stream of unborn generations at home and abroad. We show that the growth effect depends on whether the country – more generally, the trading bloc – in question is a host or source of foreign investment. Because the financing constraint plays such an important role in these economies, the link between commercial policy and foreign investment should not come as a complete surprise. But, to the best of our knowledge, no one has analyzed this link so explicitly before.

Our central contribution is to identify *dynamic trade creation*. Static trade creation is an increase in the volume of trade when the world growth rate remains unchanged; we show later that this corresponds to increased volume of trade in final goods that is the counter-part of interest income from abroad. Dynamic trade creation is an increase in the volume of trade in final goods when the world growth rate changes. Net trade creation is the sum of these two effects. Our main result is that any change in commercial policy that creates net trade enhances world growth.

In a static economy, the growth rate is given exogenously, each country's current account is balanced, and static trade creation occurs when a policy raises the volume of trade. In a dynamic economy, the world growth rate is determined endogenously, a country's current account typically is *not* balanced, and dynamic trade creation occurs when a change in distorting tariffs changes growth and affects the volume of trade. Commercial policy always has two effects in a growing world economy: it alters the volume of trade at the (fixed) original growth rate and it affects the volume of trade as world growth changes. An important contribution of this chapter is to show that the sum of these two effects is positive if and only if a change in tariffs increases a country's external surplus, induces a fall in world interest rates, and causes a rise in world growth. Thus, when moving from one second-best equilibrium to another, there is net trade creation if and only if world growth increases. We show that the static and dynamic effects always work in opposite directions, but their relative magnitudes can be determined unequivocally.

Commercial policy creates dynamic trade through its influence on the incomes and savings patterns of a trading bloc. Although our model captures the long-run behavior of a wide class of economies, its supply side has a special structure, and the final-goods sector is labor intensive. The Stolper–Samuelson Theorem then implies that a tariff on this sector raises the real wage, the source of savings. In countries that are sources of foreign investment, this policy enhances growth. But in those that host foreign investment, such a tariff reduces growth and benefits fixed factors at the expense of the current owners of capital and future generations in all countries.

Although these results are quite general, applying to all the trade structures we consider, the case of free trade areas is worth particular mention. Richardson (1995) notes that a common feature of this form of preferential trade is the proliferation of rules of origin designed to prevent arbitrage across member countries with different external tariffs. Even though these rules protect domestic producers by specifying minimum local content requirements, a free trade area that removes tariffs on internal trade in investment unambiguously reduces global protection of investment goods. This result suggests that rules of origin may be less restrictive than they appear because administrators face difficulties in disentangling current domestic content from that produced using past vintages of capital.

The rest of this chapter is structured as follows. The second section describes the model, and the third section defines a balanced growth path for the distorted world economy. The fourth section derives the direction of trade, and it examines the growth effects of both most-favored-nation tariffs and the formation of customs unions. The fifth section analyses protection-reducing and protection-enhancing free trade areas. The sixth section suggests directions for future research and argues that all our results are much more robust than the assumptions of specific utility functions and production functions might lead the reader to believe.

2. THE MODEL

We use the model of overlapping generations developed by Fisher (1992, 1995); its supply side is in the spirit of the models of Jones and Manuelli (1990) and Rebelo (1991). In each country in any period, there are two generations, the young and the old. In the initial period, the old generation lives only for one period and finances consumption from the ownership of the economy's inherited stock of capital. Every other agent is endowed with one unit of labor when young and nothing else. This agent lives for two periods and saves some of his wage in order to purchase capital and finance consumption when old.

There are n countries and two goods. In keeping with the Heckscher–Ohlin paradigm, we assume that technologies are identical across countries. Country j has a fixed number of agents per generation, L^j,[3] and its capital stock at time t is K_t^j. The first sector produces the consumption good, and the second produces the investment good. As in the literature (Ethier and Horn, 1984; Richardson, 1995), each sector can be thought of as a composite of many goods, some imported and others exported. The consumption aggregate comprises all the final

---

[3] It is simple to generalize our results to the case where all countries' populations are increasing at the same exogenous rate.

goods that create utility for agents in the world economy; output of the consumption good in country j at time t is

$$Q^j_{t,1} = \left(K^j_{t,1}\right)^\theta \left(L^j_{t,1}\right)^{1-\theta}, \tag{1}$$

where $K^j_{t,1}$ is the input of capital and $L^j_{t,1}$ is that of labor. The investment aggregate consists of intermediate goods that increase the world's capital stock. Its output is

$$Q^j_{t,2} = \Gamma K^j_{t,2}, \tag{2}$$

where the input is analogous.

All goods and factor markets are perfectly competitive, so each factor is fully employed. The full employment conditions in country j are

$$L_{t,1} \le L^j \quad \text{and} \quad k^j_{t,1} + k^j_{t,2} \le k^j_t. \tag{3}$$

Capital in the jth country follows the transition equation

$$k^j_{t+1} = Q^j_{t,2} + Z^j_t, \tag{4}$$

where Z^j_t are imports of investment goods into country j at time t. We are implicitly assuming that capital depreciates completely. This assumption underscores the notion that a period corresponds to the working life of the typical agent. Although we treat this reproducible factor as physical capital, it could just as well be any accumulable input whose private and social rates of return are equal.

Trade in investment goods is different from trade in financial claims. The pattern of *ownership* of firms in each period is determined by the disparate saving decisions of all the agents in the world economy. In the model of overlapping generations, (perpetually) imbalanced trade is the norm, not the exception.[4] In international economics, it is best to think of these as models of pure absorption. A country with a high savings rate has a relatively low propensity to spend from current income, and it will tend thus to run surpluses on current account. In a growing world economy, this means that it will acquire net foreign assets in each

---

[4] This is an old (if poorly understood) point. David Gale (1971) showed that perpetual trade imbalances arise because countries earn interest on net foreign assets, but the current account was balanced in each period in his model. Fisher (1990) emphasized that trade imbalances can arise solely because of government policies. Of course, in a model of endogenous growth, because new assets are being created in every period, countries can run perpetual trade deficits and permanent current account surpluses!

generation. We now turn our attention to the determinants of savings in the world economy.

An agent in country j born at time 0 has preferences given by

$$u^{j,0}(c_1^{j,0}) = \log c_1^{j,0}, \tag{5a}$$

and the analogous agent born at time $t \geq 1$ has the utility function

$$u^{j,t}(c_t^{j,t}, c_{t+1}^{j,t}) = (1 - \sigma^j) \log c_t^{j,t} + \sigma^j \log c_{t+1}^{j,t}, \tag{5b}$$

where $c_t^{j,s}$ is the consumption at time t of an agent born at time s in country j. Since σ^j is the marginal propensity to save from permanent income, the preferences described by Equation (5b) entail that the savings rate is independent of the real interest rate. This assumption is not without loss of generality, but it makes for a simple description of the balanced growth path in terms of the savings rates and commercial policies of each country.

Let $P_{t,i}$ be the *border* price in period t of good i. Also, let τ_i^j be country j's constant gross *ad valorem* tariff rate on good $i \in \{1, 2\}$; thus, the domestic price of good i is $\tau_i^j P_{t,i}$.[5] The numeraire is the consumption good in the first period and $P_{1,1} \equiv 1$. Hence, all prices are present prices, $p_t \equiv P_{t,1}/P_{t,2}$ is the relative world price of the consumption good in period t, and $1 + i_{t+1} \equiv P_{t,1}/P_{t+1,1}$ is the world real interest rate from periods t to $t + 1$.

Firms in sector $i \in \{1, 2\}$ choose their inputs of capital and labor to maximize profits in each period. Let W_t^j and R_t^j be the present value of the wage and rentals rates, respectively, in country j at time t. Also, let $k_{t,1}^j$ be the capital–labor ratio in the first sector in that country at that time. Then equilibrium in the factor markets implies

$$\tau_1^j P_{t,1} \theta (k_{t,1}^j)^{\theta-1} \leq R_t^j \quad \text{and} \quad \tau_2^j P_{t,2} \Gamma \leq R_t^j, \tag{6}$$

with equality if either output is strictly positive. Also,

$$\tau_1^j P_{t,1} (1 - \theta)(k_{t,1}^j)^{\theta} \leq W_t^j, \tag{7}$$

again with equality if output of the consumption good is strictly positive. If both consumption and investment outputs are strictly positive,

---

[5] We make the assumption of constant tariffs because we are interested in their long-run growth effects. Varying tariff rates across time would have transitional effects on the relative price of the consumption good in each country and on the real interest rate in the world economy.

then inequalities (6) imply

$$k_{t,1}^j = (\theta \tau^j p_t / \Gamma)^{1/1-\theta},\tag{8}$$

where $\tau^j \equiv \tau_1^j / \tau_2^j$ is the relative rate of protection in sector 1 in country j and is unity under free trade. Equation (8) is the standard relationship between domestic relative prices and resource allocation between sectors.

We can now describe the consumer's choices. The old in country j in period 1 choose $c_1^{j,0}$ to maximize Equation (5a) subject to the present value budget constraint

$$\tau_1^j c_1^{j,0} \leq R_1^j k_1^j,\tag{9a}$$

where k_1^j is the stock of capital per worker owned by the original residents of country j. Equation (9a) says that an old person in period 1 buys consumption at the local price and has income from rents on the capital. Each young agent is endowed with one unit of labor. He chooses $(c_t^{j,t}, c_{t+1}^{j,t})$ to maximize Equation (5b) subject to

$$\tau_1^j \left(P_{t,1} c_t^{j,t} + P_{t+1,1} c_{t+1}^{j,t} \right) \leq W_t^j.\tag{9b}$$

In each period, the young purchase investment goods to finance consumption in the final period of their lives. No term having to do with capital enters Equation (9b) because investment entails no profits in equilibrium.[6]

The utility function (5a) and budget constraint (9a) imply that

$$c_1^{j,0} = R_1^j k_1^j / \tau_1^j,\tag{10a}$$

and Equations (5b) and (9b) imply that the consumption profile of a person born in period $t \geq 1$ is

$$(c_t^{j,t}, c_{t+1}^{j,t}) = \left((1 - \sigma^j) W_t^j / \tau_1^j P_{t,1}, \ \sigma^j W_t^j / \tau_1^j P_{t,1} \right).\tag{10b}$$

This completes the specification of the model. The next section defines an equilibrium for the distorted economy and uses the

---

[6] We have created a model that captures in chiaroscuro Pasinetti's (1962) distinction between the savings propensities of workers and capitalists. Of course, our model is in contrast with his, because the marginal propensity of capitalists to save is zero and all savings is accomplished by workers, the owners of the fixed factors of production. Still, Pasinetti, among many others, neglected to recognize that many capitalists start out as workers and acquire assets during the course of their lives. Our model is apposite precisely because the decision to acquire capital is indeed a central part of the development process.

market-clearing conditions to derive expressions for the real interest rate and growth rate along a balanced growth path.

3. BALANCED GROWTH PATHS

Let $W_t = (W_t^1, \ldots, W_t^n)$ and $R_t = (R_t^1, \ldots, R_t^n)$ be the list of country-specific wage and rentals rates at time t and $\lambda^j \equiv L^j / \sum_{j=1}^n L^j$ be country j's constant share of the world population. Then consumption and investment per worker in the world economy are

$$c_t = \sum_{j=1}^n \lambda^j \left(c_t^{j,t-1} + c_t^{j,t}\right),$$

and

$$q_t = \sum_{j=1}^n \lambda^j Q_{t,2}^j / L^j.$$

A thorny issue in any general equilibrium model with distorting taxes is how to redistribute the tariff revenues in a neutral manner. This issue becomes very complicated in a model with overlapping generations, where society's marginal propensity to save is influenced by how the government disburses tariff revenues. We follow Rebelo (1991, p. 505) and impose that tariff revenues are used to finance the provision of public goods that have no effect on individuals' savings decisions or the production possibilities of the private sector in any country.[7] In effect, this assumption isolates the effects of fiscal policy from the distorting effects of tariffs. We justify this assumption in three ways. First, tariff revenues are a very small share of national income in most modern industrial economies.[8] Second, there is no practical transparent link between tariff revenues and fiscal policies designed to affect national savings rates. Third, since there is only one consumption aggregate in this model, the redistribution of tariff revenues will not distort the pattern of consumption, but fiscal policy, in the guise of redistribution of these revenues, certainly will influence an economy's savings and

---

[7] Until now, these distorting taxes could have been easily interpreted as import or export subsidies. In the rest of the chapter, we are explicitly assuming that any government must actually raise revenues from its distortionary policies. Since we are analyzing equilibria in which the local demand and the local supply for intermediate investment good are equal, it is best now to think of these revenues as arising from a broad aggregate of tariffs on final consumption goods.

[8] In 1995, revenues from custom duties and fees were about $19 billion in the United States, where GDP was near $7200 billion. Indeed, the interest payments on the national debt were greater than $232 billion, more than ten times national tariff revenues.

growth rates. Thus Rebelo's assumption is particularly appealing in a model of overlapping generations.

Let the vector of consumption and investment tariffs be $\tau = (\tau_1^1, \tau_2^1, \ldots, \tau_1^n, \tau_2^n)$. Given these distortions, an *equilibrium for the world economy* is a sequence of prices $\{(P_{t,1}, P_{t,2}, W_t, R_t)\}_{t=1}^{\infty}$ and corresponding aggregate quantities $\{(c_t, q_t)\}_{t=1}^{\infty}$ such that (i) Equations (1), (2), and (3) describe each country's production and resource constraints; (ii) Equations (10a) and (10b) give each agent's consumption decisions; (iii) Equations (6) and (7) relate factor prices and intensities; and (iv) Equation (4) describes the law of motion for each country's capital stock, taking as given the initial ownership of capital $(k_1^1, \ldots, k_1^n)$.

A *balanced growth path* is an equilibrium for the world economy in which all countries' gross domestic products grow at the same rate. Then $k_t = \sum_{j=1}^{n} \lambda^j k_t^j$ gives capital per worker in the world economy at time t. On a balanced growth path, the gross growth rate of capital per worker is a constant independent of time. Because each country's share of world wealth is a constant, countries with relatively high savings rates acquire a disproportionate share of the new assets created in each period. They run perpetual current account surpluses.

Since the tariffs are constant through time, intertemporal arbitrage implies that

$$P_{t,2} = \Gamma P_{t+1,2}, \qquad (11)$$

where Γ is the marginal efficiency of investment. Thus, the decline in the present price of the investment good is determined by the marginal rate of transformation between capital in periods t and $t + 1$.

The relationship between savings and investment is

$$\sum_{j=1}^{n} \lambda^j \sigma^j W_t^j = \sum_{j=1}^{n} \lambda^j \tau_2^j P_{t,2} k_{t+1}^j. \qquad (12)$$

This equation shows that each agent born in generation t spends a fraction σ^j of the present value of his permanent income on the purchase of capital. Using Equations (6), (7), (8), and (11), we can show that Equation (12) implies the following relationship between the gross growth rate of the stock of capital G and the interest rate:

$$G \equiv k_{t+1}/k_t = (p_t/p_{t-1})^{1/1-\theta} = [\Gamma/(1 + i_t)]^{1/1-\theta}. \qquad (13)$$

Because the marginal efficiency of investment is fixed at Γ, an increase in growth can occur only if real interest rates fall and firms absorb the increased outflow of capital.

Using Equations (7), (8), (10b), and (13), we can write country j's imports of the consumption good m_t^j as

$$m_t^j = \left(p_t \tau^j \theta / \Gamma\right)^{\frac{\theta}{1-\theta}} \left((1-\theta)\sigma^j \Gamma / G - \Phi^j\right), \qquad (14)$$

where $\Phi^j \equiv 1 - (1-\sigma^j)(1-\theta) > 0$. Now let the world excess demand for imports be $M_t(\tau, G) \equiv \sum_{j=1}^n \lambda^j m_t^j$, where the dependence on the tariffs and the world growth rate is explicit. The market-clearing condition for the consumption good in period t is

$$M_t(\tau, G) = (p_t \theta / \Gamma)^{\frac{\theta}{1-\theta}} \sum_{j=1}^n \lambda^j (\tau^j)^{\frac{\theta}{1-\theta}} \left(\sigma^j (1-\theta)\Gamma / G - \Phi^j\right) = 0. \tag{15}$$

It is important to note that Equation (15) is independent of P_t, the international relative price the consumption good. Markets clear for any P_t; thus, tariffs do not have the usual static term-of-trade effects, but Equation (13) shows instead that the rate of change of the terms of trade captures the model's essential growth effect. Solving Equation (15) for the growth rate yields[9]

$$G = \frac{(1-\theta)\Gamma \sum_{j=1}^n \lambda^j (\tau^j)^{\theta/1-\theta} \sigma^j}{\sum_{j=1}^n \lambda^j (\tau^j)^{\theta/1-\theta} \Phi^j}. \tag{16}$$

The gross growth rate of the world's physical stock of capital is an increasing function of the marginal efficiency of investment, and it is a smooth function of any country's *relative* tariff. Thus, the equilibrium illustrates a dynamic version of Lerner's symmetry theorem: if there are no income effects, a tariff on the consumption good is equivalent to an export tax on the investment good. Showing the existences of a

---

[9] Equation (16) assumes implicitly that all countries have strictly positive outputs of both goods in each period. A sufficiently large consumption tariff can induce a country to specialize in the consumption good, but full employment implies that there can never be complete specialization in the investment good. One can show that the condition for complete specialization is independent of time and, hence, that there is a balanced growth path where some countries produce only consumption goods. If such specialization occurs in country j, then $k_{t,1}^j = k_t^j$ and Equation (16) is changed accordingly to reflect the lower rate of growth of the world economy. Also, marginal increases in country j's consumption tariff will have no effect on the world growth rate.

balanced growth path for an arbitrary array of distorting tariffs, Equation (16) is an important contribution of this chapter. To the best of our knowledge, no other paper has been able to determine explicitly the world growth rate for an arbitrary specification of a second-best equilibrium. Furthermore, it is worth emphasizing here that the equilibrium is a balanced growth path; because all production in both sectors and preferences is so simple, there are no transition dynamics in this model.

Finally, Equation (13) implies that $1 + i_{t+1} = \Gamma/G^{1-\theta}$; thus, on a balanced growth path the real interest rate is a constant that is strictly greater than G^θ, the growth rate of world consumption. Hence, the distributive inefficiency that arises from tariffs as distorting taxes is the usual static one, even though a tariff in any country has a fundamental effect on the growth rate of the entire world economy.

4. DYNAMIC TRADE CREATION AND THE GROWTH EFFECTS OF CUSTOMS UNIONS

It is useful to examine the link between a country's trade pattern and its savings behavior. Substituting Equation (16) into Equation (14) yields

$$m_t^j = \frac{\displaystyle\sum_{i=1}^{n} \lambda^i (\tau^i)^{\theta/1-\theta} (\sigma^j \Phi^i - \sigma^i \Phi^j)}{\displaystyle\sum_{i=1}^{n} \lambda^i (\tau^i)^{\theta/1-\theta} \sigma^i} (k_{t,1}^j)^\theta. \tag{17}$$

Consider an equilibrium with free trade. Then $\tau^j = 1$, and $\Phi^j = \theta + \sigma^j(1 - \theta)$ for all j. Let $\tilde{\sigma} = \sum_{i=1}^{n} \lambda^i \sigma^i$ be the average savings rate in the undistorted world economy. Then Equation (17) reduces to $m_t^j = \theta(k_{t,1}^j)^\theta(\sigma^j - \tilde{\sigma})/\tilde{\sigma}$, and a country with an above-average savings rate imports the consumption aggregate under free trade. The term $\theta(k_{t,1}^j)^\theta$ is the share of world consumption output that accrues to capital, and $(\sigma^j - \tilde{\sigma})/\tilde{\sigma}$ is net foreign assets per capita. Thus the analog of Equation (17) corresponds exactly to country j's interest income from abroad, and it ties down the pattern of trade in the world economy. Recall that a high-savings country runs a perpetual current account surplus in a growing world economy.[10] Since imports of the consumption aggregate just offset interest income from abroad, a high-savings country imports

---

[10] Since each generation saves a constant fraction of its wage income, country j's current account surplus at time t is $(G^\theta - 1)(1 - \theta)\theta(k_{t-1,1}^j)^\theta(\sigma^j - \tilde{\sigma})/\tilde{\sigma}$ in an undistorted world economy.

the consumption good. These imports are simply the interest payments on net foreign assets that accrue to its older generation. Likewise, in an equilibrium distorted by tariffs, a country with a high value of σ^j/Φ^j serves analogously as a source of outward investment and growth. Whether a country is a source or host for foreign investment is crucial in understanding the effects of tariffs on the world economy.

We can now formally define static and dynamic trade creation. Since country j's imports depend on its tariffs and the world growth rate, differentiation of Equation (14) shows

$$\frac{dm^j/m^j}{d\tau^j/\tau^j} = \frac{\partial m^j/m^j}{\partial \tau^j/\tau^j} + \left(\frac{\partial m^j/m^j}{\partial G/G}\right)\left(\frac{dG/G}{d\tau^j/\tau^j}\right). \tag{18}$$

The first partial derivative on the right side of Equation (18) holds the growth rate constant and defines *static trade creation*. In a model of exogenous growth, this is the only kind of trade creation, because commercial policy *ipso facto* has no effect on the growth rate. The second term on the right side of Equation (18) defines *dynamic trade creation*. This partial derivative holds country j's tariffs constant, and the total derivative captures the overall increase in the world growth owing to a change in that distortion.

Logarithmic differentiation of Equation (14) shows that $(\partial m^j/m^j)/(\partial \tau^j/\tau^j) = \theta/(1-\theta) > 0$. Thus, static trade creation is a positive constant; it captures the Stolper–Samuelson effect in this model. Consider a 1% increase in τ^j. The magnification effect implies that real wages rise by $\theta/(1-\theta)\%$. At fixed real interest rates, Equation (10b) shows that country j's marginal propensity to consume from permanent income is unity; thus, aggregate consumption also rises by $\theta/(1-\theta)\%$. Also, Equation (8) shows that capital per worker in that sector rises by $1/(1-\theta)\%$. Finally, Equation (1) shows that output per worker rises by $\theta/(1-\theta)\%$. Thus, *static trade creation occurs if a source country for foreign investment raises its tariff on consumer goods or if a host country for foreign investment raises its tariff on investment goods*. Because this expression does not depend on any of the distortions in the world economy, it serves to underscore that even the static effects of tariff changes in a growth model are fundamentally different from the usual static effects that have been explored before. Static trade creation occurs because interest payments from net foreign assets increase. Even if the growth rate is unchanged, the share of net foreign assets owned by a high-savings country will increase. At constant world interest (and, thus, growth) rate, this country will import more of the consumption good.

What about the dynamic effects of tariffs? Differentiation of Equation (16) and some algebra using Equations (8), (14), and (17) show that

$$
\frac{dG/G}{d\tau^j/\tau^j} = \frac{\lambda^j m_t^j (\tau^j)^{\theta/1-\theta}}{(k_{t,1}^j)^\theta \sum_{i=1}^{n} \lambda^i (\tau^i)^{\theta/1-\theta} \Phi^i} \left(\frac{\partial m_t^j/m_t^j}{\partial \tau^j/\tau^j} \right). \tag{19}
$$

Thus, world growth increases if and only if a source country for foreign investment raises its tariff on consumption goods or a host country for foreign investment raises its tariff on investment goods. The intuition is that the Stolper–Samuelson effects in a static model have growth effects when world savings depend on the distribution of income in the world economy. Moreover, a bit more algebra implies

$$
\left(\frac{\partial m^j/m^j}{\partial G/G} \right) \left(\frac{dG/G}{d\tau^j/\tau^j} \right) = -\frac{\lambda^j \sigma^j (\tau^j)^{\theta/1-\theta}}{\sum_{i=1}^{n} \lambda^i (\tau^i)^{\theta/1-\theta} \sigma^i} \left(\frac{\partial m_t^j/m_t^j}{\partial \tau^j/\tau^j} \right).
$$

Hence, dynamic trade creation has the opposite sign from static trade creation, but its magnitude is smaller. Also, dynamic trade creation depends on all the distortions in the world economy, and it is particularly strong for a large country.

What is the economic intuition? Consider a source country for foreign investment that raises its tariff on consumption goods. The static effect creates trade, since the change in distortions raises the real income of and, thus, interest payments to the fixed factors (namely, the savers) in a country importing consumption goods. Also, the change in commercial policy raises world growth, so in the long run agents everywhere in the world will be better off. But some of that increase in growth is at the expense of a lower volume of trade in final goods, because the surplus country has a lower than average rate of absorption and acquires more net foreign assets on the new growth path.

What have we shown? *If a change in tariffs creates net trade, it raises world growth.* Notice that there are two ways to create net trade. We have already explored the first: a surplus country can raise its tariff on final consumption goods. But there is a second possibility: a deficit country can raise its tariff on intermediate investment goods. This result is really quite general. We have focused on second-best equilibria in a model that captures the general properties of growing economies where economies of scale do not come into play and agents do not live forever. In this class of models, net trade creation is synonymous with increases in economic growth. This result is the second fundamental contribution of this chapter.

It is straightforward to apply the preceding analysis to customs unions. Since each economy has a standard concave production frontier, the supply curve in each sector is upward sloping. Thus, if countries in a union trade with countries outside the bloc, the relative price in any member is determined by the common external tariff.[11] Hence, the effects of customs union formation are captured by changing the various tariffs to a common external tariff. Then the union's effect on world growth depends on whether it increases the average rate of protection of the consumption sector.

Let $U \subset \{1, \ldots, n\}$ be the index set of the countries forming the customs union and suppose that the union imposes a common external relative consumption tariff τ^0, while removing all internal trade barriers. A customs union increases the average rate of protection of the consumption sector if and only if

$$(\tau^0)^{\frac{\theta}{1-\theta}} > \sum_{j \in U} \lambda^j (\tau^j)^{\frac{\theta}{1-\theta}} / \sum_{j \in U} \lambda^j. \tag{20}$$

If the members had the same relative tariffs τ^j, then Inequality (20) collapses to $\tau^o > \tau^j$.

Again, the growth effects of customs union formation depend on the presence of dynamic trade creation. Suppose that the countries in the union were a net source of foreign investment in the original distorted equilibrium. Then Equations (15) and (19) imply that growth increases if and only if Inequality (20) holds. Increased protection of consumption raises the share of income going to the high savers in the world economy, and the customs union creates an excess supply of investment and raises growth. On the other hand, if the union chose a high common external *investment* tariff, then the resulting excess

---

[11] Thus, we need not be concerned with the special case analyzed by Wonnacott and Wonnacott (1981), in which the formation of a customs union causes one of the members to switch all of its exports of a good from the rest of the world to its partners. Also, because the supply curves are upward sloping, we will not have the type of trade diversion that occurs in models with perfectly elastic supply when all of one partner's imports are switched from outside the bloc to a union partner.

demand for investment slows growth. These results are reversed if the bloc had the opposite trade pattern in the original equilibrium. Finally, Equation (19) implies that any union has a strong effect on world growth if it is large or if the marginal efficiency of investment is high.

5. THE GROWTH EFFECTS OF A FREE TRADE AREA

Our analysis of free trade areas makes use of the important insight of Richardson (1995). He shows that producer prices will be equalized across countries within the free trade area even if rules of origin prevent consumer arbitrage between partner countries. This simple but valuable observation is employed by Grossman and Helpman (1995) to narrow the number of interesting outcomes from the formation of a free trade area down to three cases. They refer to these as *enhanced protection*, *reduced protection*, and *intermediate protection*, a combination of the first two.

Assume that countries j and k are partners in the free trade area. We follow Grossman and Helpman in focusing on protection of a single good; however, we do not impose their small-country assumption. The interesting cases involve commodities that are imported by at least one of the partners. Without loss of generality, assume that the consumption tariff rate in j is not lower than that in k; thus, $\tau_1^j \geq \tau_1^k$.

Before the formation of the free trade area, consumers and producers in j and k face prices $\tau_1^j P_{t,1}$ and $\tau_1^k P_{t,1}$, respectively. If j's demand for consumption at $\tau_1^j P_{t,1}$ exceeds total output in the free trade area, then j will import consumption goods from the rest of the world at $\tau_1^j P_{t,1}$, the common producer price in the bloc. All of k's consumption output is exported to j, while all consumption in k is imported from the rest of the world at the lower price $\tau_1^k P_{t,1}$. Thus, for given world prices, producer and consumer prices in j and consumer prices in k are unaffected by the free trade area, but producers in k receive greater protection than before. This is Grossman and Helpman's enhanced protection case.

In contrast, if, at the lower price $\tau_1^k P_{t,1}$, the combined output in the free trade area exceeds the demand for consumption in j, then the consumer and producer price in both countries will be driven down to $\tau_1^k P_{t,1}$, the reduced protection case. Now the free trade area is equivalent to a fall in j's most-favored-nation consumption tariff.

The intermediate case arises if there exists a price between $\tau_1^j P_{t,1}$ and $\tau_1^k P_{t,1}$ at which j's demand for consumption is exactly satisfied by the combined outputs of j and k. This situation is essentially a combination of the reduced and enhanced protection cases. For our purposes, sufficient insight can be obtained by focusing on the two polar cases. However, it is necessary to make clear what is meant by these two cases in the presence of terms-of-trade effects and in a dynamic framework.

Incorporating terms-of-trade effects is straightforward. Simply define enhanced and reduced protection as before with the world prices taken at their market-clearing levels in each period. However, the complication arising from a dynamic analysis is potentially more troublesome. For example, a case of enhanced protection may later switch to one of reduced protection. Fortunately, the same regime applies for all time.

To see this, consider now the case of a free trade area between j and k. Let

$$\Delta_t \equiv \lambda^j \left(k_{t,1}^j\right)^\theta + \lambda^k \left(k_{t,1}^j\right)^\theta - \lambda^j \left(c_t^{j,t-1} + c_t^{j,t}\right) < 0 \qquad (21)$$

define the enhanced protection case. The term $\lambda^k (k_{t,1}^j)^\theta$ makes explicit that output of the consumption good in country k now depends on producer prices in country j. Since $\Delta_t = \lambda^k (k_{t,1}^j)^\theta - m_t^j$, it follows from Equation (17) that $\Delta_t/(k_{t,1}^j)^\theta$ is independent of t. Thus the condition in Equation (21) is independent of time.

Likewise,

$$\Psi_t \equiv \lambda^j \left(k_{t,1}^k\right)^\theta + \lambda^k \left(k_{t,1}^k\right)^\theta - \lambda^j \left[c_t^{j,t-1}(\tau^k, p_t) + c_t^{j,t}(\tau^k, p_t)\right] > 0 \qquad (22)$$

defines the reduced protection case, where now firms in both countries produce using the capital–labor ratio $k_{t,1}^k$. Now the terms $c_t^{j,t-1}(\tau^k, p_t)$ and $c_t^{j,t}(\tau^k, p_t)$ show that consumers in j face the consumption price in k. Since Equation (8) implies that $k_{t,1}^j / k_{t,1}^k$ is independent of t, one can show analogously that $\Psi_t/(k_{t,1}^k)^\theta$ and, hence, Equation (22) are also independent of time. Continuity establishes the analogous fact for the regime of intermediate protection. Hence, a free trade area will stay in the same regime.

We first consider a free trade area that involves changes in consumption tariffs. Again, the reduced protection case for consumption is equivalent to country j's lowering its most-favored-nation relative tariff to τ_1^k/τ_2^j. Thus the growth effects of the free trade area depend on whether j was a host or a source of foreign investment in the original distorted equilibrium. If j had been a host of foreign investment, the positive growth effects are captured by Equation (19). Otherwise, the free trade area slows growth. These effects are significant if the marginal efficiency of investment is high or if country j itself is large.

The case of a free trade area that gives rise to enhanced consumption protection is less straightforward. Now producer prices in k are higher than consumer prices there, and the term for m_t^k in Equation (15) is replaced by

$$(p_t \tau^j \theta / \Gamma)^{\frac{\theta}{1-\theta}}\left((1-\theta)(\tau_1^j/\tau_1^k)(\sigma^k(\Gamma/G) + (1-\sigma^k)) - 1\right).$$

Since $\tau_1^j \geq \tau_1^j$, the partial derivative of this expression with respect to τ^j is positive if country k imports the consumption good before the advent of the free trade area. In this case, a protection-enhancing policy raises world growth. Thus, a sufficient uncondition for such a free trade area to raise growth is that the *low-tariff* partner was originally a source of foreign investment.

We consider second a free trade area that changes investment tariffs. The situation is different for trade in these goods. *A free trade area necessarily entails a regime of reduced protection for investment goods.* The argument is by contradiction. Let $\tau_2' \equiv \min\{\tau_2^j, \tau_2^k\}$ and $\tau_2'' \equiv \max\{\tau_2^j, \tau_2^k\}$ be the minimum and maximum of the two relevant investment tariffs. Suppose there is an equilibrium with enhanced protection for investment. Then "consumer" and producer prices for investment in one country are $\tau_2'' P_{t,2}$, while the consumer price of the investment in the other country is $\tau_2' P_{t,2}$ and the producer price there is $\tau_2'' P_{t,2}$. Of course, the consumer price of the intermediate investment good is what firms pay to acquire an increment to their capital stock, whereas its producer price is what a firm in the investment-goods sector earns by selling it.

Consider buying a machine in the country with the high investment tariff and then renting out the increment to the capital stock in the next period; such a transaction earns unity in present prices because it is a simple risk-free way to transfer income across periods. But a producer in the low-tariff country can also buy an investment good from the rest of the world and use the incremental capital to produce investment goods for resale in the trading partner's market. This transaction yields a return of $\tau_2'' P_{t+1,2} \Gamma / \tau_2' P_{t,2} > 1$, since the price of the investment good in the trading partner's market is $\tau_2'' P_{t+1,2}$. Of course, this situation is inconsistent with equilibrium, even when rules of origin ensure protection of local intermediate goods.

Hence, reduced protection of the investment good will mean that the appropriate relative tariffs become τ_1^j / τ_2' and τ_1^k / τ_2', and the country with the formerly higher investment tariff now experiences an increase in its τ^j. Thus, world growth increases if and only if that country was a source of foreign direct investment in the original distorted equilibrium. The unifying principle is this: a free trade area increases world growth if and only if it increases the bloc's imports of consumption, yielding a world excess supply of investment and an equilibrating fall in interest rates.

6. CONCLUSION

Our work can answer some broad empirical questions with minimal data. For example, it is possible to predict that a preferential trading arrangement will cause dynamic trade creation and, hence, increased world growth simply by knowing the bloc's pattern of trade, trade barriers, national populations, savings ratios, and direction of foreign investment. Most of these data are readily available. If one also knows the technological parameters and tariff revenues, then it is possible to calculate explicit growth effects for each case we have analyzed.

Although we have pursued positive questions, our analysis has strong normative implications for the welfare effects of the formation of preferential trading arrangements. Calculating the full effects of tariffs in a dynamic framework, however, requires deriving the transition path, whereas we have confined ourselves to balanced growth. An evaluation of a free trade area might contrast the long-run growth effects against the usual short-run static effects. An exercise comparable to that performed by Baldwin (1992) would reveal the relative magnitudes of these two considerations.

We might emphasize that our results do not depend on the specific production functions (1) and (2) and utility functions (5a) and (5b). There are three crucial elements that determine the balanced growth path: the marginal efficiency of investment, the income share of the fixed factor, and the marginal propensity to save from permanent income. Let $f_2(k_{t,2}^j)$ be the intensive form of investment production; then define $\lim_{k_{t,2}^j \to \infty} f_2'(k_{t,2}^j) \equiv \Gamma$, and all the properties about the marginal efficiency of investment used in describing the balanced growth path are still true. Likewise, let $f(k_t)$ be any neoclassical production function; then the sequence $\{k_{t,1}^j f_1'(k_{t,1}^j)/f_1(k_{t,1}^j)\}_{t=1}^{\infty}$ has at least one accumulation point because capital's share is between zero and one. Let this accumulation point be θ^j and set $\theta = \sum_{j=1}^{n} \lambda^j \theta^j$; then the growth rate would still not exceed $(1 - \theta)\Gamma$, just as Equation (16) shows.

How general is our assumption about utility function (5b)? As long as preferences are smooth, one can always define a savings rate from permanent income; this rate might depend on the real interest rates in the world economy. Still, on a balanced growth path, there would be some constant real interest rate and some corresponding savings propensity so that an analog of Equation (13) describes the growth rate. Thus, any entirely general specification of a neoclassical economy with two sectors would help describe the transitional effects of commercial policy, and a general specification of our model might have multiple equilibria with balanced growth. But in the long run, the growth effects of trade policies would be much as we have described.

The assumption that agents live for only two periods might seem restrictive. However, what really matters is not that agents live for two periods but rather that the fixed factor that we have called labor is used intensively in the consumption-goods sector. Then protecting that sector raises the share of income that accrues to savers in that country. How this affects the world savings rate is the essence of our analysis. Any theory of endogenous growth that takes seriously the notion that people do not live forever must confront the fact that they acquire an arbitrarily large amount of the capital from finite streams of income. Thus, it is not the fact that agents live for two periods that matters, but it is crucial that tariffs have simple general equilibrium effects on the distribution of income.

On the other hand, our assumption about the redistribution of tariff revenues matters quite a bit. National generational surpluses or deficits indeed affect the growth rate of the world economy, as Fisher (1994) has emphasized. Still, we isolated the effects of commercial policy from policies that redistribute income across generations. It is then a robust result in a wide class of models that increased relative consumption tariffs raise the real income of fixed factors. Then the growth effect of commercial policy depends on whether the country in question is a source of outward foreign investment.

REFERENCES

Baldwin, Richard E. (1992), "Measurable Dynamic Gains from Trade," *Journal of Political Economy* 100: 162–74.

Boldrin, Michele (1992), "Dynamic Externalities, Multiple Equilibria, and Growth," *Journal of Economic Theory* 58: 198–218.

Ethier, W., and H. Horn (1984), "A New Look at Economic Integration," in H. Kierzkowski (ed.), *Monopolistic Competition and International Trade*, Clarendon Press, Oxford.

Fisher, Eric O'N (1990), "Sustainable Balance of Trade Deficits," *Journal of Monetary Economics* 25: 411–30.

Fisher, Eric O'N (1992), "Sustained Growth in the Model of Overlapping Generations," *Journal of Economic Theory* 58: 77–92.

Fisher, Eric O'N (1994), "Crowding Out in a Model of Endogenous Growth," Unpublished Working Paper, Ohio State University.

Fisher, Eric O'N (1995), "Growth, Trade and International Transfers," *Journal of International Economics* 39: 143–58.

Gale, David (1971), "General Equilibrium with Imbalance of Trade," *Journal of International Economics* 1: 141–58.

Galor, Oded (1992), "A Two-Sector Overlapping-Generations Model: A Global Characterization of the Dynamical System," *Econometrica* 60: 1351–86.

Grossman, Gene M., and Elhanan Helpman (1991), *Innovation and Growth in the Global Economy*, MIT Press, Cambridge, MA.

Grossman, Gene M., and Elhanan Helpman (1995), "The Politics of Free Trade Agreements," *American Economic Review* 85: 667–90.

Jones, Larry E., and Rodolfo Manuelli (1990), "A Convex Model of Equilibrium Growth: Theory and Policy Implications," *Journal of Political Economy* 98: 1008–38.

Jones, Larry E., and Rodolfo Manuelli (1992), "Finite Lifetimes and Growth," *Journal of Economic Theory* 58: 171–97.

Kehoe, Timothy J. (1994), "Assessing the Economic Impact of North American Free Trade," in M. Delal Baer and Sidney Weintraub (eds.), *The NAFTA Debate: Grappling with Unconventional Trade Issues*. Lynne Reiner Publishers, Boulder, CO.

Lucas, Robert E., Jr. (1988), "On the Mechanics of Economic Development," *Journal of Monetary Economics* 22: 3–42.

Pasinetti, L. (1962), "Rate of Profit and Income Distribution in Relation to the Rate of Economic Growth," *Review of Economic Studies* 29: 267–79.

Ramsey, Frank P. (1928), "A Mathematical Model of Saving," *Economic Journal* 38: 543–59.

Rebelo, Sergio (1991), "Long-Run Policy Analysis and Long-Run Growth," *Journal of Political Economy* 99: 500–21.

Richardson, Martin (1995), "Tariff Revenue Competition in a Free Trade Area," *European Economic Review* 39: 1429–37.

Rivera-Batiz, Luis A., and Paul M. Romer (1991), "Economic Integration and Endogenous Growth," *Quarterly Journal of Economics* 106: 531–55.

Srinivasan, T. N. (1964), "Optimal Savings in a Two Sector Model of Growth," *Econometrica* 32: 358–73.

Uzawa, H. (1964), "Optimal Saving in a Two Sector Model of Growth," *Review of Economic Studies* 31: 1–24.

Wonnacott, P., and R. Wonnacott (1981), "Is Unilateral Tariff Reduction Preferable to a Customs Union? The Curious Case of the Missing Foreign Tariffs," *American Economic Review* 71: 704–14.

Young, Alwyn (1991), "Learning by Doing and the Dynamic Effects of International Trade," *Quarterly Journal of Economics* 106: 369–405.

7

Substitutability of Capital, Investment Costs, and Foreign Aid

Santanu Chatterjee and Stephen J. Turnovsky

1. INTRODUCTION

Public investment is widely accepted as being a crucial determinant of economic growth. Interest in the impact of public capital on private capital accumulation and economic growth originated with the seminal theoretical work of Arrow and Kurz (1970) and the more recent empirical research of Aschauer (1989a, 1989b).[1] Most of the subsequent literature has focused on closed economies, using both the Ramsey model and the AK endogenous growth framework (see, e.g., Futagami et al., 1993; Glomm and Ravikumar, 1994; Baxter and King, 1993; Fisher and Turnovsky, 1998). Turnovsky (1997a) extends Futagami et al.'s work to a small open economy and introduces various forms of distortionary taxation, as well as the possibility of both external and internal debt financing. Devarajan et al. (1998) address the issue of whether public capital should be provided through taxation or through granting subsidies to private providers.[2]

A critical issue, especially in poor, resource-constrained developing countries, concerns how the new investment in infrastructure is financed. One significant source for funding such investment is external

---

[1] See Gramlich (1994) for a comprehensive survey of the recent empirical literature.
[2] The efficient use of infrastructure is a further important issue. For example, Hulten (1996) shows that inefficient use of infrastructure accounts for more than 40% of the growth differential between high- and low-growth countries.

This paper was written to honor the contributions of John Pitchford, an innovative scholar, who, among other things, produced the first published analysis of the CES production function. Stephen Turnovsky looks back with pleasure to the 1970s when John and he were colleagues at the Australian National University and enjoyed many fruitful collaborations. The authors would like to thank three anonymous readers for their comments. This research was supported in part by the Castor Endowment at the University of Washington. In addition, Chatterjee gratefully acknowledges financial support from the Grover and Creta Ensley Fellowship.

financing. This may be in the form of borrowing from abroad, through bilateral or multilateral loans, or through unilateral capital transfers, in the form of tied grants or official development assistance, as recently observed in the European Union (EU). Faced with below-average per capita incomes and low growth rates among some of its joining members, the EU introduced pre-accession aid programs to assist these and other potential member nations in their transition into the union.[3] This process of "catching up" began in 1989 with a program of unilateral capital transfers from the EU through the Structural Funds program, and subsequent programs were introduced in 1993 and in 2000. These assistance programs tied the capital transfers (or grants) to the accumulation of public capital and were aimed at building up infrastructure in the recipient nation. The objective of these aid programs was for the recipient economy to attain strong positive growth differentials relative to the EU average in the short run, and thereby achieve higher and sustainable living standards in alignment with EU standards, and ultimately to gain accession to EU membership.

In a recent paper, Chatterjee et al. (2003) have analyzed the process of developmental assistance in the form of tied-capital transfers to a small growing open economy. One critical assumption adopted in that analysis is that the underlying production function is of the Cobb–Douglas form in private and public capital. While this functional form is prevalent throughout much of the recent endogenous growth literature, it is of course restrictive (see Lucas, 1988; Barro, 1990; Futagami et al., 1993; Bond et al., 1996; Turnovsky, 1997a, 1997b). In particular, it suffers from the serious shortcoming that the resulting impact of the transfer on the growth performance is predicated on the intratemporal elasticity of substitution between these two forms of capital being assumed to be unity. Intuitively, one would expect the impact of a tied transfer to be highly sensitive to the degree of intratemporal substitution between these two types of capital inputs. To analyze this, one needs to employ a more flexible production specification, such as the constant elasticity of substitution (CES) production function, which accommodates alternative degrees of substitution. This is the task

---

[3] Greece, Ireland, Spain, and Portugal were recipients of unilateral capital transfers tied to public investment projects under the Structural Funds Program between 1989 and 1993 and 1993 and 1999. A similar tied transfer program, called Agenda 2000, has been initiated for eleven aspiring member nations (central Eastern European countries) and is expected to continue until 2006 (see European Union, 1998a, 1998b).

undertaken in this chapter. Indeed, as our analysis will confirm, the elasticity of substitution is an important determinant of both the dynamic adjustment paths generated by a program of tied transfers and their welfare implications.

The CES production function has a long history, being initially introduced by Pitchford (1960) and Arrow et al. (1961). The original specification was in terms of capital and raw labor, and extensive empirical evidence on the elasticity of substitution between these two inputs was produced during the 1960s and 1970s. Berndt (1976) provides a reconciliation between alternative estimates for the aggregate production function, concluding that estimates generally range between around 0.8 and 1.2. In a recent panel study of 82 countries over a 28-year period, Duffy and Papageorgiou (2000) find that they can reject the Cobb–Douglas specification for the entire sample in favor of the more general CES production function. They also report that the degree of substitution between inputs (in their case human and physical capital) may vary with the stages of development. For example, there is a higher degree of substitutability of inputs in rich countries than in poor countries, a feature absent from the Cobb–Douglas specification. Empirical evidence on the substitutability of public and private capital is sparse. Lynde and Richmond (1993) introduce public and private capital into a more general translog production function for UK manufacturing and find that the Cobb–Douglas specification is rejected.

Factor substitution can occur intratemporally and/or intertemporally. Whereas the former is incorporated by the CES production function, the latter may be captured by the introduction of differential costs of adjustment, along the lines associated with Hayashi (1982). Indeed, the impact of foreign aid on the evolution of the economy depends not only on the short-run degree of substitutability between the two types of capital but also on their relative costs of adjustment.

This chapter attempts to bridge the gap between the development literature on the impact of foreign aid and the growth literature on the role of public investment, in the context of a growing open economy that receives development assistance in the form of foreign aid from the rest of the world. Specifically, our chapter contributes to the aforementioned branches of literature in two important directions. First, we consider aid in the form of tied unilateral capital transfers, i.e., funds to be used by the recipient for the specific purpose of creating public capital.[4] As Brakman and van Marrewijk (1998) point out, in the post–World War II era, unilateral capital transfers have increasingly taken the form of development assistance or foreign aid. This is important when one recognizes that between two-thirds and three-fourths of official development assistance to infrastructure is fully or partially tied.[5] On the other hand, most of the existing development literature, which examines the possible effects of aid on saving and investment in developing countries, has been based mainly on static models.[6] In contrast, we embed the aid flow in an intertemporal optimization framework characterized by endogenous growth, which enables us to compare both the short-run and the long-run effects of tied and untied aid on the dynamic evolution and growth rate of the economy and, ultimately, on welfare.[7]

Second, since it is likely that external assistance and borrowing will fail to meet the total financial needs for public investment, domestic participation by both the government and the private sector is also important. Recently, in a panel study of 56 developing countries and six four-year periods (1970–93), Burnside and Dollar (2000) find that foreign aid is most effective when combined with a positive policy environment in the recipient economy. In earlier works, Gang and Khan (1990) and Khan and Hoshino (1992) report that most bilateral aid for public investment in lesser developed countries (LDCs) is tied and is given on the condition that the recipient government invests certain resources into the same project. We specifically characterize

---

[4] Bhagwati (1967) points out that tied assistance may take different forms. The transfer or aid from abroad may be linked to (i) a specific investment project, (ii) a specific commodity or service, or (iii) to procurement in a specific country. We focus our analysis on the first type of tying, i.e., to an investment project. Examples of such tied capital transfers include the relocation of German capital equipment at the end of the Second World War to Eastern Europe and the Soviet Union, the Marshall Plan in the post–World War II era for the reconstruction of Europe, and, more recently, the European Union's pre-accession aid programs for aspiring member nations.

[5] World Bank (1994).

[6] See Cassen (1986) and, more recently, Brakman and van Marrewijk (1998) for a survey of this literature. Two exceptions include Djajic et al. (1999) and Hatzipanayotou and Michael (2000), who examine the effects of transfers in an intertemporal context.

[7] This issue is also related to the pure "transfer problem," one of the classic issues in international trade, and dates back to Keynes (1929) and Ohlin (1929). Recent contributions include Bhagwati et al. (1983), Galor and Polemarchakis (1987), Turunen-Red and Woodland (1988), and Djajic et al. (1999). For a comprehensive survey of the literature, see Brakman and van Marrewijk (1998). Our analysis differs from this literature by focusing on "productive" (tied) transfers, the use of which is tied to public investment.

the consequences of domestic cofinancing of public investment and outline the trade-offs faced by a recipient government when it responds optimally to a flow of external assistance from abroad.

In addition to the CES specification of technology, the model we employ has the following key characteristics. First, external assistance is tied to the accumulation of public capital, which is therefore an important stimulus for private capital accumulation and growth. Second, new investment in both types of capital is subject to convex costs of installation. Allowing for differential costs of investment for public and private capital raises the issue of how the degree of substitutability between the two capital stocks interacts with installation costs in determining the effect of a tied foreign aid shock. Third, we assume that public investment in infrastructure is financed both by the domestic government as well as via the flow of international transfers, thereby incorporating the important element of domestic cofinancing, characteristic of most bilateral aid programs that are tied to specific public investment projects. The international transfers are assumed to be tied to the scale of the recipient economy and therefore are consistent with maintaining an equilibrium of sustained (endogenous) growth in that economy.

We also assume that the small open economy faces restricted access to the world capital market in the form of an upward-sloping supply curve of debt, according to which the country's cost of borrowing depends on its debt position relative to its total capital stock, the latter serving as a measure of its debt-servicing capability. This assumption is motivated by the large debt burdens of most developing countries, which give rise to the potential risk of default on international borrowing. Indeed, evidence suggesting that more indebted economies pay a premium on their loans from international capital markets to insure against default risk has been provided by Edwards (1984). An interesting question, therefore, is whether barriers to international borrowing have any implications for the welfare effects of foreign aid programs.

The main results of our model are the following. The effect of an increase in foreign aid depends critically on whether it is tied or untied. An untied aid program does not generate any dynamic response, but instead leads to instantaneous increases in consumption and welfare. On the other hand, an aid program that is tied to investment in public capital generates a transitional dynamic adjustment in the recipient economy. The magnitude and the direction of the transitional dynamics and long-run effects depend crucially on the elasticity of substitution between the two types of capital in the recipient economy. Our analysis suggests that tied aid is more effective in terms of its impact on long-run growth and welfare for countries that have low substitutability between factors of production. This finding has important policy implications, especially in light of recent empirical evidence suggesting that less-developed or poor countries have elasticities of substitution that are significantly below unity. We find that the welfare gains from a particular type of aid program (tied or untied) are sensitive to the costs of installing public capital and capital market imperfections, even for small changes in the degree of substitutability between inputs. Economies in which the elasticity of substitution between the two types of capital and the installation costs are relatively high are likely to find tied transfers to be welfare-deteriorating. For such economies, untied aid will be more appropriate.

The rest of the chapter is organized as follows. The analytics of the theoretical model are laid out in Section 2. Section 3 presents a numerical analysis of the impact of a foreign aid shock and the resulting transitional dynamics. Section 4 briefly addresses the issue of cofinancing, and Section 5 discusses the sensitivity of intertemporal welfare to the elasticity of substitution, investment costs, and capital market imperfections. Section 6 presents some concluding remarks.

2. THE ANALYTICAL FRAMEWORK

2.1. Private Sector

We consider a small open economy populated by an infinitely lived representative agent who produces and consumes a single traded commodity. Output Y of the commodity is produced using the CES production function

$$Y = \alpha \left[\eta K_G^{-\rho} + (1 - \eta) K^{-\rho} \right]^{-1/\rho}, \qquad \alpha > 0, \quad 0 < \eta < 1, \quad \rho > -1, \tag{1a}$$

where K denotes the representative agent's stock of private capital, K_G denotes the stock of public capital, and $\sigma \equiv 1/(1 + \rho)$ is the elasticity of substitution between private and public capital in production. The model abstracts from labor so that private capital should be interpreted broadly to include human as well as physical capital (see Rebelo, 1991).

The agent consumes this good at the rate C, yielding utility over an infinite horizon represented by the isoelastic utility function[8]

$$U \equiv \int_0^\infty \frac{1}{\gamma} C^\gamma e^{-\beta t} dt, \qquad -\infty < \gamma < 1. \tag{1b}$$

The agent also accumulates physical capital, with expenditure on a given change in the capital stock, I, involving adjustment (installation) costs specified by the quadratic (convex) function

$$\psi(I, K) = I + h_1 \frac{I^2}{2K} = I\left(1 + h_1 \frac{I}{2K}\right). \tag{1c}$$

This equation is an application of the familiar cost-of-adjustment framework, where we assume that the adjustment costs are proportional to the *rate* of investment per unit of installed capital (rather than its level). The linear homogeneity of this function is necessary for a steady-state equilibrium having ongoing growth to be sustained. The net rate of capital accumulation is, thus,

$$\dot{K} = I - \delta_K K, \tag{1d}$$

where δ_K denotes the rate of depreciation of private capital.

Agents may borrow internationally on a world capital market. The key factor we wish to take into account is that the creditworthiness of the economy influences its cost of borrowing from abroad. Essentially we assume that world capital markets assess an economy's ability to service debt costs and the associated default risk, the key indicator of which is the country's debt–capital (equity) ratio. As a result, the interest rate that countries are charged on world capital markets increases with this ratio. This leads to the upward-sloping supply schedule for debt, expressed by assuming that the borrowing rate, $r(N/K)$, charged on (national) foreign debt, N, relative to the stock of private capital, K, is of the form

$$r(N/K) = r^{\cdot} + \omega(N/K), \qquad \omega' > 0, \tag{1e}$$

where $r^{\cdot}$ is the exogenously given world interest rate and $\omega(N/K)$ is the country-specific borrowing premium that increases with the nation's

---

[8] The exponent γ is related to the intertemporal elasticity of substitution s, by $s = 1/(1 - \gamma)$, where $\gamma = 0$ is equivalent to a logarithmic utility function.

debt–capital ratio. The homogeneity of the relationship is required to sustain a balanced growth equilibrium.[9]

The agent's decision problem is to choose consumption, and the rates of accumulation of capital and debt, to maximize intertemporal utility (1b) subject to the flow budget constraint

$$\dot{N} = C + r\left(\frac{N}{K}\right)N + \Psi(I, K) - (1 - \tau)Y + \overline{T}, \qquad (2)$$

where N is the stock of debt held by the private sector, τ is the income tax rate, and $\overline{T}$ denotes lump-sum taxes.[10] It is important to emphasize that, in performing his optimization, the representative agent takes the borrowing rate $r(.)$ as given. This is because the interest rate facing the debtor nation, as reflected in its upward-sloping supply curve of debt, is a function of the economy's *aggregate* debt–capital ratio, which the individual agent assumes he is unable to influence.

The optimality conditions with respect to C and I are, respectively,

$$C^{\gamma-1} = \nu \qquad (3a)$$

$$1 + h_1\left(\frac{I}{K}\right) = q, \qquad (3b)$$

where ν is the shadow value of wealth in the form of internationally traded bonds, q' is the shadow value of the agent's private capital stock, and $q = q'/\nu$ is defined as the market price of private capital in terms of the (unitary) price of foreign bonds. The first of these conditions equates the marginal utility of consumption to the shadow value of wealth, while the latter equates the marginal cost of an additional unit of investment, which is inclusive of the marginal installation cost

---

[9] A rigorous derivation of Equation (1e) presumes the existence of risk. Because we do not wish to model a full stochastic economy, we should view equation (1e) as representing a convenient reduced form, one supported by empirical evidence; see, e.g., Edwards (1984), who finds a significant positive relationship between the spread over LIBOR (e.g., $r\cdot$) and the debt-to-GNP ratio. Eaton and Gersovitz (1989) provide formal justifications for relationship (1e). Various formulations can be found in the literature. The original formulation by Bardhan (1967) expressed the borrowing premium in terms of the absolute stock of debt; see also Obstfeld (1982) and Bhandari et al. (1990). Other authors such as Sachs (1984) also argue for a homogeneous function such as Equation (1e). We have also considered the Edwards (1984) formulation, $r = r(N/Y)$, and results very similar to those reported are obtained.

[10] It is natural for us to assume $N > 0$ so that the country is a debtor nation. However, it is possible for $N < 0$ to occur, in which case the agent accumulates credit by lending abroad. For simplicity, interest income is assumed to be untaxed.

$h_1 I/K$, to the market value of capital. Equation (3b) may be immediately solved to yield the following expression for the rate of private
capital accumulation:

$$\frac{\dot{K}}{K} \equiv \phi_K = \frac{q-1}{h_1} - \delta_K. \tag{3b'}$$

Applying the standard optimality conditions with respect to N and K
implies the usual arbitrage relationships, equating the rates of return on
consumption and investment in private capital to the costs of borrowing
abroad:

$$\beta - \frac{\dot{v}}{v} = r\left(\frac{N}{K}\right) \tag{4a}$$

$$\frac{(1-\tau)(1-\eta)\alpha\left[\eta(K_G/K)^{-\rho} + (1-\eta)\right]^{-(1+\rho)/\rho}}{q} + \frac{\dot{q}}{q} + \frac{(q-1)^2}{2h_1 q}$$

$$-\delta_K = r\left(\frac{N}{K}\right). \tag{4b}$$

Finally, in order to ensure that the agent's intertemporal budget constraint is met, the following transversality conditions must hold:

$$\lim_{t\to\infty} v B e^{-\beta t} = 0, \qquad \lim_{t\to\infty} q' K e^{-\beta t} = 0. \tag{4c}$$

2.2. Public Capital, Transfers, and National Debt

The resources for the accumulation of public capital come from two
sources: domestically financed government expenditure on public capi-
tal, $\overline{G}$, and a program of capital transfers, TR, from the rest of the world.
We therefore postulate

$$G \equiv \overline{G} + \lambda TR, \qquad 0 \le \lambda \le 1,$$

where λ represents the degree to which the transfers from abroad
are tied to investment in the stock of public infrastructure. The case
$\lambda = 1$ implies that transfers are completely tied to investment in public
capital, representing a "productive" transfer. In the other polar case,
$\lambda = 0$, incoming transfers are not invested in public capital and, hence,
represent a "pure" transfer of the Keynes–Ohlin type.

We assume that the gross accumulation of public capital, G, is also subject to convex costs of adjustment, similar to that of private capital[11]

$$\Omega(G, K_G) = G\left(1 + \left(\frac{h_2}{2}\right)\left(\frac{G}{K_G}\right)\right).$$

In addition, the stock of public capital depreciates at the rate δ_G, so the net rate of public capital accumulation is

$$\dot{K}_G = G - \delta_G K_G. \tag{5}$$

To sustain an equilibrium of ongoing growth, both domestic government expenditure on infrastructure ($\overline{G}$) and the flow of transfers from abroad must be tied to the scale of the economy:

$$\overline{G} = \overline{g}Y \quad \text{and} \quad TR = \theta Y, \quad 0 < \overline{g} < 1, \quad \theta > 0, \quad 0 < \overline{g} + \theta < 1.$$

We can therefore rewrite Equation (5) in the following form:

$$\dot{K}_G = G - \delta_G K_G = gY - \delta_G K_G = (\overline{g} + \lambda\theta) Y - \delta_G K_G$$

$$g = \overline{g} + \lambda\theta > 0, \tag{5'}$$

and, dividing Equation (5) by K_G, the growth rate of public capital is given by

$$\frac{\dot{K}_G}{K_G} \equiv \phi_G = (\overline{g} + \lambda\theta)\frac{Y}{K_G} - \delta_G. \tag{6}$$

The government sets its tax and expenditure parameters to continuously maintain a balanced budget:

$$\tau Y + TR + \overline{T} = \Omega(G, K_G). \tag{7}$$

The national budget constraint, or the nation's current account, can be obtained by combining Equations (7) and (2):

$$\dot{N} = r\left(\frac{N}{K}\right)N + C + \Psi(I, K) + \Omega(G, K_G) - Y - TR. \tag{8}$$

Equation (8) states that the economy accumulates debt to finance its total expenditures on public capital, private capital, consumption, and interest payments net of output produced and transfers received. It is immediately apparent that higher consumption or investment raises the rate at which the economy accumulates debt. The direct

---

[11] Noting the definition of G, we see that the transfers contribute to the financing of the installation costs as well as to the accumulation of the new public capital.

effect of a larger unit transfer on the growth rate of debt is given by $(\lambda - 1) + (h_2/K_G)\lambda G$. An interesting observation is that the more that transfers are tied to public investment (the higher λ), the lower is the decrease in the growth rate of debt. When transfers are completely tied to investment in infrastructure, i.e., $\lambda = 1$, debt increases due to higher installation costs. However, the indirect effects induced by the change will still need to be taken into account.

2.3. Macroeconomic Equilibrium

The steady-state equilibrium has the characteristic that all real quantities grow at the same constant rate and that q, the relative price of capital, is constant. Therefore, we shall express the dynamics of the system in terms of the following stationary variables, normalized by the stock of private capital: $c \equiv C/K$, $k_g \equiv K_G/K$, $n \equiv N/K$, and q. The equilibrium system is derived as follows.

First, taking the time derivative of k_g and substituting Equations (6) and (3b') yields

$$\frac{\dot{k}_g}{k_g} \equiv \phi_G - \phi_K = \alpha \, (\bar{g} + \lambda\theta) \left[\eta + (1 - \eta) \, k_g^\rho \right]^{-1/\rho}$$

$$- \frac{q - 1}{h_1} - (\delta_G - \delta_K). \tag{9a}$$

Next, dividing Equation (8) by N, and substituting, we can rewrite Equation (8) as

$$\phi_N = r\,(n) + \frac{1}{n} \left[\{(\bar{g} + \lambda\theta) - (1 + \theta)\} \, y + \frac{q^2 - 1}{2h_1} \right.$$

$$\left. + \frac{h_2}{2} \, (\bar{g} + \lambda\theta)^2 \, \frac{y^2}{k_g} + c \right], \tag{8'}$$

where $y = Y/K = \alpha \left[\eta k_g^{-\rho} + (1 - \eta) \right]^{-1/\rho}$. Taking the time derivative of n and combining with Equation (3b') leads to

$$\frac{\dot{n}}{n} \equiv \phi_N - \phi_K = r\,(n)$$

$$+ \frac{1}{n} \left[\{(\bar{g} + \lambda\theta) - (1 + \theta)\} \, y + \frac{q^2 - 1}{2h_1} + \frac{h_2}{2} \, (\bar{g} + \lambda\theta)^2 \, \frac{y^2}{k_g} + c \right]$$

$$- \left(\frac{q - 1}{h_1} \right) + \delta_K. \tag{9b}$$

Third, from Equations (3a) and (4a), we derive the growth rate of consumption,

$$\frac{\dot{C}}{C} = \phi_C = \frac{r\,(n) - \beta}{1 - \gamma}.$$

Taking the time derivative of c and combining with the preceding expression leads to

$$\frac{\dot{C}}{C} \equiv \phi_C - \phi_K = \frac{r\,(n) - \beta}{1 - \gamma} - \frac{q-1}{h_1} + \delta_K. \tag{9c}$$

Finally, rewriting Equation (4b) implies

$$\dot{q} = [r\,(n) + \delta_K]q - \alpha\,(1 - \tau)\,(1 - \eta)\left[\eta k_g^{-\rho} + (1 - \eta)\right]^{-(1+\rho)/\rho}$$
$$- \frac{(q-1)^2}{2h_1}. \tag{9d}$$

Equations (9a)–(9d) provide an autonomous set of dynamic equations in k_g, n, c, and q from which the steady-state equilibrium can be derived.

2.4. Steady-State Equilibrium

The economy reaches a steady state when $\dot{k}_g = \dot{n} = \dot{c} = \dot{q} = 0$, implying that $\dot{K}/K = \dot{K}_G/K_G = \dot{N}/N = \dot{C}/C \equiv \tilde{\phi}$, the steady-state growth rate of the economy. The steady state is thus described by

$$\alpha\,(\bar{g} + \lambda\theta)\left[\eta + (1 - \eta)\,\tilde{k}_g^{\rho}\right]^{-1/\rho} - \delta_G = \frac{\tilde{q} - 1}{h_1} - \delta_K \tag{10a}$$

$$r\,(\tilde{n}) + \frac{1}{\tilde{n}}\left[\{(\bar{g} + \lambda\theta) - (1 + \theta)\}\tilde{y} + \frac{\tilde{q}^2 - 1}{2h_1} + \frac{h_2}{2}\,(\bar{g} + \lambda\theta)^2\,\frac{\tilde{y}^2}{\tilde{k}_g} + \tilde{c}\right]$$
$$= \left(\frac{\tilde{q} - 1}{h_1}\right) - \delta_K \tag{10b}$$

$$[r\,(\tilde{n}) + \delta_K]\tilde{q} - \alpha\,(1 - \tau)\,(1 - \eta)\left[\eta\tilde{k}_g^{-\rho} + (1 - \eta)\right]^{-(1+\rho)/\rho}$$
$$- \frac{(\tilde{q} - 1)^2}{2h_1} = 0 \tag{10c}$$

$$\frac{r(\tilde{n}) - \beta}{1 - \gamma} = \frac{\tilde{q} - 1}{h_1} - \delta_K = \tilde{\phi}. \qquad (10d)$$

Equations (10a)–(10d) determine the steady-state equilibrium in the following recursive manner. First, Equations (10a), (10c), and (10d) jointly determine $\tilde{k}_g, \tilde{q}, \tilde{r}(.)$, and $\tilde{\phi}$ such that the equilbrium growth rates of public capital, private capital, and consumption are all equal and that the rate of return on private capital equals the borrowing costs. Having determined $\tilde{r}$ and $\tilde{k}_g$, the equilibrium stock of debt–capital ratio, $\tilde{n}$, is obtained from Equation (1e). Given $\tilde{k}_g, \tilde{q}, \tilde{r}(.)$, and $\tilde{n}$ (and recalling the definition of y), the equilibrium consumption–capital ratio, $\tilde{c}$, is obtained from the current account equilibrium condition (10b). Provided $\tilde{r} > \tilde{\phi}$ (which, we shall show, is required for the transversality condition to hold), higher marginal borrowing costs reduce total interest payments, raising the consumption–capital ratio. Also, higher installation costs h_2 reduce the amount of output available for consumption, $\tilde{c}$. Because this system is highly non-linear, it need not be consistent with a well-defined steady-state equilibrium with $\tilde{k}_g > 0, \tilde{c} > 0$. Our numerical simulations, however, yield well-defined steady-state values for all plausible specifications of all the structural and policy parameters of the model.[12]

It is seen that the transfers impinge on the equilibrium through the growth of public capital (10a) and the goods market equilibrium (10b). Setting $\lambda = 0$, we see from Equations (10a), (10c), and (10d) that $\tilde{k}_g, \tilde{q}, \tilde{r}(.)$, and $\tilde{\phi}$ are all independent of the level of untied transfers θ, an increase in which is fully reflected in steady-state consumption. If the transfers are tied, they will lead to an increase in the steady-state ratio of public to private capital, growth rate, and debt–capital ratio by an amount that depends on the elasticity of substitution. In the extreme case of perfect substitutability between the two types of capital ($\rho = -1$), $\tilde{q}, \tilde{r}(.)$, and $\tilde{\phi}$ are all independent of θ, while k_g increases.

2.5. Equilibrium Dynamics

Equations (9a)–(9d) form the dynamics of the system in terms of k, n, q, and c. Linearizing these equations around the steady-state values of

---

[12] A discussion of issues pertaining to nonexistent or multiple equilibria in a related model is provided by Turnovsky (2000); similar issues apply here.

k_g, n, q, and c obtained from Equations (10a)–(10d),

$$
\begin{pmatrix} \dot{k}_g \\ \dot{n} \\ \dot{c} \\ \dot{q} \end{pmatrix} =
\begin{pmatrix}
a_{11} & 0 & 0 & -\tilde{k}_g/h_1 \\
a_{21} & r'\,(\tilde{n})\,\tilde{n} + r\,(\tilde{n}) - \tilde{\phi} & 1 & \dfrac{\tilde{q} - \tilde{n}}{h_1} \\
0 & \dfrac{r'\,(\tilde{n})\,\tilde{c}}{1-\gamma} & 0 & -\tilde{c}/h_1 \\
a_{41} & r'\,(\tilde{n})\,\tilde{q} & 0 & r\,(\tilde{n}) - \tilde{\phi}
\end{pmatrix}
\begin{pmatrix} k_g - \tilde{k} \\ n - \tilde{n} \\ c - \tilde{c} \\ q - \tilde{q} \end{pmatrix}, \quad (11)
$$

where

$$
a_{11} = \alpha^{-\rho}\,(\eta - 1)\,(\bar{g} + \lambda\theta)\,\frac{\tilde{y}^{1+\rho}}{\tilde{k}_g},
$$

$$
a_{21} = \alpha^{-\rho}\eta\,[(\bar{g} + \lambda\theta) - (1 + \theta)]\,(\tilde{y}/\tilde{k}_g)^{(1+\rho)}
$$
$$
+ h_2\alpha^{-\rho}\eta\,(\bar{g} + \lambda\theta)^2\,(\tilde{y}/\tilde{k}_g)^{(2+\rho)} - \frac{h_2}{2}\,(\bar{g} + \lambda\theta)^2\,(\tilde{y}/\tilde{k}_g)^2,
$$

and $a_{41} = -\alpha^{-2\rho}\eta\,(1 - \tau)\,(1 - \eta)\,(1 + \rho)\left(\tilde{y}^{1+2\rho}/\tilde{k}_g^{1+\rho}\right)$. The determinant of coefficient matrix (11) can be shown to be positive under the condition that $r(.) > \tilde{\phi}$, i.e., the steady-state interest rate facing the small open economy must be greater than the steady-state growth rate of the economy. Imposing transversality condition (4c), we see that this condition is indeed satisfied. Since matrix (11) is a fourth-order system, a positive determinant implies that there could be zero, two, or four positive (unstable) roots. However, our numerical simulations yield saddle-point behavior for all plausible ranges of parameters. Thus, dynamic system (11) is saddle-point stable with two positive (unstable) and two negative (stable) roots, the latter being denoted by μ_1 and μ_2, with $\mu_2 < \mu_1 < 0$.

3. NUMERICAL ANALYSIS OF TRANSITIONAL DYNAMICS

Due to the complexity of the model, we will employ numerical methods to examine the dynamic effects of transfers. We begin by calibrating a benchmark economy using the following parameters representative of a small open economy, which starts out from an equilibrium with zero transfers.

The Benchmark Economy

Preference parameters	$\gamma = -1.5, \beta = 0.04$
Production parameters	$\alpha = 0.4, \eta = 0.2, h_1 = 15, h_2 = 15$
Elasticity of substitution in production	$\sigma = 0.33, 1, \to \infty$
Depreciation rates	$\delta_K = 0.05, \delta_G = 0.04$
World interest rate	$\bar{r} = 0.06,$
Premium on borrowing	$\alpha = 0.1^{13}$
Policy parameters	$\tau = 0.15, \bar{g} = 0.05$
Transfers	$\theta = 0, \lambda = 0$

Our choices of preference parameters[13] β and γ, depreciation rates δ_K and δ_G, and the world interest rate $\bar{r}$ are standard, while α is a scale variable. The productive elasticity of public capital $\eta = 0.2$ is consistent with the empirical evidence (see Gramlich, 1994). The borrowing premium $\alpha = 0.10$ is chosen to ensure a plausible equilibrium national debt-to-income ratio. The tax rate is set at $\tau = 0.15$, while the rate of government expenditure on public investment is assumed to be $\bar{g} = 0.05$. The choice of adjustment costs is less obvious. Setting $h_1 = 15$ is consistent with Ortigueira and Santos (1997), who find that $h_1 = 16$ leads to a plausible speed of convergence of around 2%. Auerbach and Kotlikoff (1987) assume $h_1 = 10$, recognizing that this is at the low values of estimates, while Barro and Sala-i-Martín (1995) propose a value above 10. We have also assumed smaller values of h with little change in results. Note also that the equality of adjustment costs between the two types of capital serves as a plausible benchmark.

The critical parameter upon which we focus is the elasticity of substitution, σ, and we consider three benchmark economies, depending on the degree of substitutability between public and private capital in production. These include (i) low elasticity of substitution, $\sigma = 0.33$ (Table 1A); (ii) unitary elasticity of substitution, $\sigma = 1$ (Table 1B); and (iii) perfect substitutability between the two types of capital, where $\sigma \to \infty$ (Table 1C). Benchmark (ii) represents the familiar Cobb–Douglas production function, while (i) and (iii) represent two extreme cases, where there is very little or extremely high degree of substitutability in production.

---

[13] The functional specification of the upward-sloping supply curve that we use is $r(n) = \bar{r} + e^{an} - 1$. Thus, in the case of a perfect world capital market, when $a = 0, r = \bar{r}$, the world interest rate.

The calibrated benchmark economy derived from the preceding parameter specification is reported in Table 1. The standard case of the Cobb–Douglas specification is reported in Table 1B, row 1. It implies a steady-state ratio of public to private capital of 0.29; the consumption–output ratio is 0.60, and the debt-to-GDP ratio of 0.45, leading to an equilibrium borrowing premium of 1.42% over the world rate. The capital–output ratio is over 3, with the equilibrium growth rate being around 1.37%. This equilibrium is a reasonable characterization of a small medium-indebted economy experiencing a modest steady rate of growth and having a relatively small stock of public capital.

Tables 1A–1C reveal the sensitivity of the steady-state equilibrium to variations in the elasticity of substitution in production. For a very low degree of substitution in production, $\sigma = 0.33$ (Benchmark I, Table 1A, row 1), the steady-state ratio of public to private capital is increased to 0.437, the interest rate is 2.4% – *lower* than the world interest rate of 6% – which implies that this economy is a net creditor to the rest of the world and, thus, has an initial current account surplus. This is reflected in a debt–output ratio of –1.24. The low elasticity of substitution causes agents to lower their investment in the stock of private capital and enjoy higher consumption, leading to a consumption–output ratio of 0.78. Due to the low investment in private capital and high consumption, the steady-state growth rate in this economy is –0.6%.

In the extreme case of perfect substitutability between public and private capital (Benchmark III, Table 1C, row 1), the equilibrium ratio of public to private capital decreases to 0.27. The consumption–output ratio decreases to 0.51 and the current account deficit increases, reflected in a higher debt-to-GDP ratio of 1.11 and a steady-state interest rate of 9.87%. The high elasticity of substitution leads to an equilibrium growth rate of 2.35%.

3.1. A Permanent Foreign Aid Shock: Long-Run Effects

We now consider a permanent increase in foreign aid flows to the aforementioned benchmark specifications. Specifically, the transfer from abroad is tied to the scale of the economy and increases from 0% of gross domestic product (GDP) in the initial steady state to 5% of GDP in the new steady state (an increase in θ from 0 to 0.05). However, this aid may be tied to new investment in public capital ($\lambda = 1$), representing the case of a "productive" transfer, or it may be untied

Table 1. Responses to a permanent transfer shock

	$\tilde{k}_g$	$\tilde{r}\%$	C^τ/Y	N^τ/Y	$\phi_K(0)\%$	$\phi_G(0)\%$	$\phi_Y(0)\%$	$\phi_C(0)\%$	$\tilde{\phi}\%$	$\Delta(W)\%$
A. Benchmark I: low substitutability in production ($\sigma = 0.33$)										
$\theta = 0$, $\lambda = 0$, $\overline{g} = 0.05$, $\tau = 0.15$	**0.437**	**2.42**	**0.778**	**-1.24**	**-0.60**	**-0.60**	**-0.60**	**-0.60**	**-0.60**	–
Tied transfer										
$\theta = 0.05$, $\lambda = 1$, $\overline{g} = 0.05$, $\tau = 0.15$	0.696	7.04	0.643	0.29	1.04	2.73	1.99	-0.60	1.22	+50.0
Pure transfer										
$\theta = 0.05$, $\lambda = 0$, $\overline{g} = 0.05$, $\tau = 0.15$	0.437	2.42	0.828	-1.24	-0.6	-0.60	-0.60	-0.60	-0.60	+6.42
B. Benchmark II: unitary substitutability in production ($\sigma = 1$)										
$\theta = 0$, $\lambda = 0$, $\overline{g} = 0.05$, $\tau = 0.15$	**0.291**	**7.42**	**0.60**	**0.45**	**1.37**	**1.37**	**1.37**	**1.37**	**1.37**	–
Tied transfer										
$\theta = 0.05$, $\lambda = 1$, $\overline{g} = 0.05$, $\tau = 0.15$	0.61	8.84	0.561	0.774	1.70	6.74	2.71	1.37	1.938	+9.83
Pure transfer										
$\theta = 0.05$, $\lambda = 0$, $\overline{g} = 0.05$, $\tau = 0.15$	0.291	7.42	0.651	0.45	1.37	1.37	1.37	1.37	1.37	+8.32
C. Benchmark III: perfect substitutability in production ($\sigma \cong \infty$)										
$\theta = 0$, $\lambda = 0$, $\overline{g} = 0.05$, $\tau = 0.15$	**0.269**	**9.87**	**0.509**	**1.11**	**2.35**	**2.35**	**2.35**	**2.35**	**2.35**	–
Tied transfer										
$\theta = 0.05$, $\lambda = 1$, $\overline{g} = 0.05$, $\tau = 0.15$	0.577	9.87	0.513	1.04	2.08	8.69	2.50	2.35	2.35	-2.43
Pure transfer										
$\theta = 0.05$, $\lambda = 0$, $\overline{g} = 0.05$, $\tau = 0.15$	0.269	9.87	0.559	1.11	2.35	2.35	2.35	2.35	2.35	+9.82

Table 2. *Sensitivity of permanent responses to the elasticity of substitution*

	$d\bar{k}_g$	$d\bar{q}$	$d\bar{r}\%$ pts	$d(C^{\gamma}/Y)$	$d(N^{\gamma}/Y)$	$d\bar{\phi}$	$\Delta(W)\%$
$\sigma = 0.1$	0.113	0.32	5.26	−0.122	1.599	2.10	70.93
$\sigma = 0.5$	0.300	0.21	3.49	−0.108	1.071	1.39	32.10
$\sigma = 0.8$	0.318	0.12	1.96	−0.059	0.501	0.78	14.81
$\sigma = 1$	**0.319**	**0.09**	**1.42**	**−0.040**	**0.322**	**0.57**	**9.83**
$\sigma = 1.2$	0.319	0.07	1.09	−0.029	0.218	0.44	6.96
$\sigma = 1.5$	0.318	0.05	0.79	−0.019	0.130	0.32	4.45
$\sigma = 4$	0.312	0.01	0.22	−0.002	−0.023	0.09	−0.36
$\sigma \cong \infty$	0.308	0.00	0.00	0.004	−0.075	0.00	−2.43

($\lambda = 0$), representing the case of a "pure" transfer from abroad. The short-run and long-run responses of key variables in the recipient economy are reported in rows 2 and 3 of Tables 1A–1C, which correspond to the varying elasticity of substitution. The final column in the tables summarizes the effects on economic welfare measured by the optimized utility of the representative agent,

$$W = \int_0^{\infty} \frac{1}{\gamma} C^{\gamma} e^{-\beta t} dt,$$

where C is evaluated along the equilibrium path. These welfare changes are calculated as the percentage change in the initial stock of capital necessary to maintain the level of welfare unchanged following the particular shock. We will first discuss the long-run effects of the foreign aid shock (Tables 1 and 2) and then proceed to a discussion of the transitional dynamics generated by this shock (Figures 1–3).

3.1.1. Tied Transfer

The long-run impact of a tied aid shock is reported in row 2 of Tables 1A–1C. Since the aid is tied to new investment in public capital, the implied long-run increase in the stock of public capital increases the long-run marginal product of private capital and generates a dynamic adjustment for its market price, q. However, the magnitude and direction of the initial response of q and its consequent dynamic adjustment will depend crucially on the elasticity of substitution between the two types of capital stocks, σ.

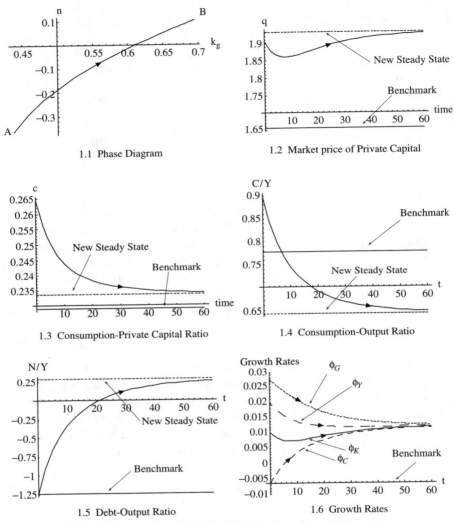

Figure 1. Low Subsitutability of Inputs: $\sigma = 0.33$.

Row 2 of Table 1B describes the standard case of the Cobb–Douglas production function. In the new steady state the ratio of public to private capital increases from 0.29 to 0.61, thereby generating a huge investment boom in infrastructure. The increase in the stock of public capital increases the marginal productivity of private capital, thereby

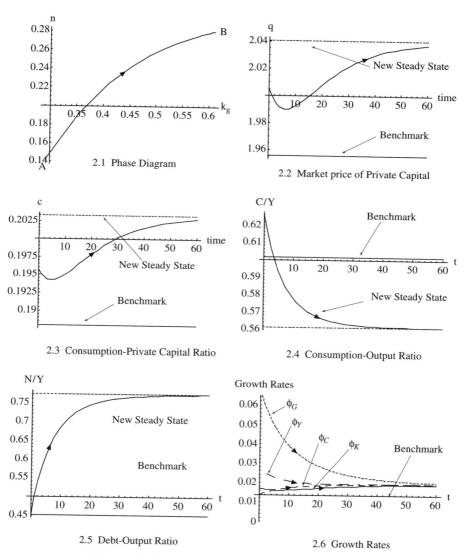

2.1 Phase Diagram

2.2 Market price of Private Capital

2.3 Consumption-Private Capital Ratio

2.4 Consumption-Output Ratio

2.5 Debt-Output Ratio

2.6 Growth Rates

Figure 2. Unitary Elasticity of Substitution: $\sigma = 1$.

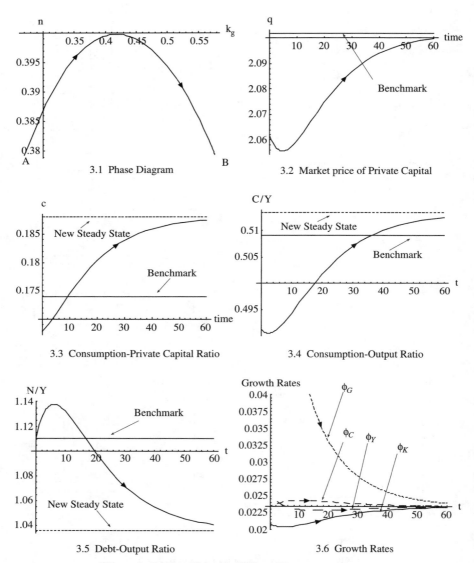

Figure 3. Perfect Substituability of Inputs: $\sigma \rightarrow \infty$.

leading to a positive, though lesser, accumulation of private capital. Although the transfer stimulates consumption through the wealth effect (like the pure transfer), the higher long-run productive capacity has a greater effect on output, leading to a decline in the long-run consumption–output ratio from 0.60 to 0.56. The higher productivity raises the long-run growth rate to 1.94%, while long-run welfare improves by 9.83%, as indicated in the last column of row 3. The increased accumulation of both private and public capital leads to a higher demand for external borrowing as a means of financing new investment in private capital and the installation costs of public capital. This results in an increase in the steady-state debt–output ratio from 0.45 to 0.77, raising the borrowing premium to over 2.8%. However, this higher debt relative to output is sustainable because it is caused by higher investment demand rather than higher consumption demand. The long-run increase in the economy's productive capacity (as measured by the higher stocks of public and private capital, and output) ensures that the higher debt is sustainable. This view has also been expressed by Roubini and Wachtel (1998).

For Benchmark I (Table 1A, row 2), since the elasticity of substitution between the two types of capital stock is very low ($\sigma = 0.33$), there is a large increase in q in order to induce the agent to increase private investment to complement the boom in public investment. The ratio of public to private capital increases from 0.44 to about 0.70. The large increase in q and the consequent investment boom turns the current account surplus into a deficit with the debt-to-GDP ratio increasing from –1.24 to 0.28 and the interest rate from 2.4 (3.6% below the world rate) to 7.04% (1.04% above the world rate). Consequently, the consumption–output ratio goes down from 0.78 to 0.64, indicating a large substitution away from consumption. The steady-state growth rate almost doubles from –0.6 to about 1.2%. There is a large long-run welfare gain of about 50%.

In Benchmark III, the polar case of perfect substitutability between public and private capital (Table 1C, row 2), the long-run change in q is zero; hence, the long-run increase in the ratio of public to private capital from 0.27 to 0.58 can be attributed mainly to the boom in public capital brought about by the tied foreign aid shock. As a result, the long-run interest rate remains unchanged. Since there is no long-run effect on q, the boom in public investment does not crowd out consumption as before, but leads to a slight increase in the consumption–output ratio from 0.50 to 0.51. Consequently, the long-run debt position of the economy improves from 1.11 to 1.04. Another effect of q not changing in the long run is that the growth rate remains unchanged at 2.35%. The tied transfer also entails a long-run welfare loss of 2.43%. However, even though the tied aid in this case does not have long-run effects on certain key variables, it does generate a dynamic adjustment that will be discussed in Section 3.2.

3.1.2. Pure Transfer

A permanent pure transfer shock, i.e., an aid flow not tied to any investment activity, does not generate any transitional adjustment, nor does it have any long-run effects on the key variables in the economy except for consumption and welfare (Tables 1A–1C, row 3). The pure transfer only raises consumption, and also long-run welfare, proportionately. For example, for Benchmark I, the consumption–output ratio goes up from 0.78 to 0.83, and from 0.60 to 0.65 for Benchmark II. For Benchmark III, it goes up from 0.51 to 0.56. However, even though long-run welfare increases due to an untied aid flow, the gains increase with the elasticity of substitution. For Benchmark I, the gain in welfare is 6.4%, while it is 8.3% and 9.8% for Benchmarks II and III, respectively.

3.2. The Effectiveness of Foreign Aid and the Elasticity of Substitution

The dependence of the efficacy of a tied aid program on the elasticity of substitution in production in the recipient country is an important question. Some indication of this is provided in the three panels of Table 1, and this is further considered in Table 2, where the range of the elasticity of substitution is expanded to cover the range $0.1 \leq \sigma \leq \infty$. The Cobb–Douglas production function is indicated in bold, whereas the shaded area reflects values of σ that lie within plausible sampling errors of $\sigma = 1$. One of the highlights of this table is that the effects of the tied transfer on the equilibrium debt–output ratio, the equilibrium growth rate, and welfare are highly sensitive to relatively minor changes in σ from this benchmark value. Thus, for example, if a researcher estimates $\sigma = 1$ with a standard error of 0.1 – a tight estimate – with 95% probability, the implied welfare gain of 9.83% could be as high as 14.8% or as low as 7%.

From Table 2 we find that, as σ increases, a tied aid program leads to generally higher long-run increases in the ratio of public to private capital and smaller increases in q. Due to the smaller increases in q as σ increases, the increase in private investment is also reduced. This leads to less borrowing, reflected by a decline in the increase in the equilibrium interest rate and debt-to-GDP ratio as σ increases. In fact, as σ approaches infinity, the current account actually improves. The crowding out of consumption also declines as σ increases, thereby reflecting lower induced private investment due to higher substitutability in production. An increase in σ also reduces the positive effect of the tied aid program on growth and welfare: the long-run gains from both growth and welfare decline as substitutability in production goes up.

The preceding results lead us to believe that, insofar as its effect on long-run growth and welfare is concerned, a tied aid program is more effective in countries with a low elasticity of substitution in production. This observation complements the recent findings of Duffy and Papageorgiou (2000) that less-developed or poor countries have elasticities of substitution that are significantly below unity and developed or richer countries have elasticities that are significantly above unity. In such a scenario, our analysis shows that a tied aid program may be more effective for poor countries than for their richer counter-parts.

3.3. Transitional Dynamics

The transitional dynamic responses of the economy to a tied aid program are illustrated in Figures 1–3, corresponding to low ($\sigma = 0.33$), Cobb–Douglas ($\sigma = 1$), and high factor substitutability ($\sigma \to \infty$), respectively. The basic phase diagram, showing the stable adjustment path in k_g–n space are graphed in Figures 1.1, 2.1, and 3.1. For low degrees of substitutability, k_g and n both increase approximately proportionately, reflecting the paths of the differential growth rates. The initial stimulus to public capital raises its initial growth rate to over 2.7%, after which it declines monotonically toward the new equilibrium of 1.2%. By contrast, private capital adjusts only gradually. Indeed, after increasing on impact to 1.04%, it declines marginally, before the stimulating effect of the higher public capital has its full impact and eventually raises its growth rate toward the equilibrium. With public capital growing uniformly faster than private capital, k_g is always increasing. The stimulus to investment and the associated resource costs

raise borrowing and, while this is mitigated by the amount of the transfer, national debt rises (or national credit falls) at a faster rate than
domestic capital, so borrowing costs rise as well. Over time, as the
growth rate of private capital catches up, borrowing costs and the need
to accumulate further debt are mitigated, and the transitional path tilts
in favor of the relative accumulation of public capital.

As the elasticity of substitution increases, the curvature of the adjustment path increases. The higher the degree of substitution between the
two types of capital, the more the transfer increases the initial growth
rate of public capital relative to that of private capital.[14] At the same
time, the rate of debt accumulation increases, raising borrowing costs.
Over time, as the growth rate of public capital declines, and that of
private capital increases, foreign borrowing and borrowing costs fall.
For a very high elasticity of substitution, we get very rapidly increasing debt and borrowing costs during the early phases of the transition.
However, over time these inhibit borrowing, which declines, and in the
limiting case where the two types of capital are perfect substitutes, n
ultimately returns to its initial level.

The contrasting transitional paths of the four growth rates ϕ_K, ϕ_G, ϕ_Y
and ϕ_C toward their common long-run growth rate are shown in Figures
1.6, 2.6, and 3.6. In all cases, the stimulus to public capital raises its
initial growth rate substantially, after which it declines monotonically.
By contrast, private capital adjusts only gradually. The growth rate of
output is an average of the growth rates of the two capital stocks. The
fact that the growth rate of output initially doubles from 1.37 to 2.72%,
in the case of the Cobb–Douglas production function, is of interest and
is consistent with the experiences of some of the recipient countries in
the EU. Finally, the growth rate of consumption is unaffected on impact
and responds only gradually. The reason for this becomes evident by
recalling the growth rate of consumption,

$$\frac{\dot{C}}{C} = \phi_C = \frac{r(n) - \beta}{1 - \gamma},$$

and the fact that it depends on the sluggishly evolving debt–capital
ratio n.

An alternative perspective on the transitional adjustment paths can
be obtained by looking at the transitional dynamics of q, the market

---

[14] Care must be exercised in comparing the slopes of the loci in Figures 1.1–1.3, because the
units vary.

price of private capital, depicted in Figures 1.2, 2.2, and 3.2. When σ is low (Figure 1.2), the initial jump in q has to be large in order to induce the required private investment to complement the long-run increase in the stock of public capital. The large increase in q results in a large initial increase in private investment, which leads to the initial decline in k_g. Thereafter, q declines toward its new steady-state level and the resultant decrease in the rate of increase of private investment causes k_g to gradually increase toward its new higher steady-state level. The same observations carry over to the case of $\sigma = 1$ (Figure 2.2). However, in this case the required initial jump in q is smaller. In the case of perfect substitutability (Figure 3.2), q decreases instantaneously to accommodate the implied boom in public investment. The consequent fall in private investment leads to the initial monotonic increase in k_g and n. However, the higher stock of public capital raises the marginal product of private capital, and eventually both q and private investment start rising. Due to perfect substitutability, the long-run increase in q must be zero; hence, q eventually returns to its initial steady-state level, and so does n – after the initial increase, it gradually declines back to its original equilibrium level.

The time paths for the consumption–capital ratio and consumption–output ratio are depicted in figures 1.3, 1.4, 2.3, 2.4, 3.3, and 3.4, respectively. For low values of σ ($= 0.33$ and 1), there is an initial upward jump in consumption due to the wealth effect created by the initial upward jump in q. Thereafter, as private capital accumulation and output increases, the consumption–capital and consumption–output ratios decline monotonically toward their respective long-run equilibrium values. However, when there is perfect substitutability of the two types of capital, the initial downward jump in q creates a negative wealth effect and the consumption–capital and consumption–output ratios jump down slightly on the incidence of the shock. However, as q gradually increases, the wealth effect becomes positive and consumption increases in transition to its new higher equilibrium level.

The dynamics for the debt-to-GDP ratio are depicted in Figures 1.5, 2.5, and 3.5. For low values of σ ($=0.33$ and 1), the implied capital accumulation increases the debt-to-GDP ratio monotonically toward its new higher steady-state level. However, in the case of perfect substitutability, the increase in the debt-to-GDP ratio is reversed due to the decrease in private capital accumulation and borrowing, and the debt position of the economy improves as the debt-to-GDP ratio now monotonically declines to its new lower steady-state level.

4. COFINANCING

Several aid programs call for cofinancing by the domestic government. In Table 3 we compare the welfare effects of the tied and pure transfers with two alternative forms of cofinancing. In the first, the government receives a tied transfer of 2.5% of its income, which it must match with an equal increase in its expenditure; in the second it must match an untied transfer. In all four cases, the economy is experiencing a 5% increase in expenditure.

For low or medium elasticity of substitution, the tied transfer (TT) is superior to the pure transfer (PT), whereas for a high σ this ordering is reversed, as we have seen. In all cases the matched tied transfer (MTT) is dominated by the TT. This is because the MTT involves making the size of the government sector too large. While the matched pure transfer (MPT) is never dominant, it is superior to the PT in the case where $\sigma = 0.33$ and it is superior to the TT as $\sigma \to \infty$.[15]

5. WELFARE SENSITIVITY TO INVESTMENT COSTS AND CAPITAL MARKET IMPERFECTIONS

While the aforementioned parameters represent a plausible description of a small poorly endowed open economy, some of the welfare implications are dependent on this characterization. Table 4 conducts some sensitivity analysis. Specifically, we compare the welfare gains from a tied and an untied aid program in response to variations in the following three factors:

(i) the cost of installing public capital (h_2);
(ii) the cost of borrowing from international capital markets (a); and
(iii) the elasticity of substitution between public and private capital (σ).

Specifically, each table addresses the following question: For a given cost of installing public capital, what are the gains from a tied and untied

---

[15] Chatterjee et al. (2003) address the question of optimal cofinancing in the case of the Cobb–Douglas production. The analogous exercise can be pursued here.

Table 3. *Cofinancing trade-offs*

	%$\Delta(W)$
A. Low substitution in production: $\sigma = 0.33$	
Tied transfer (TT) $\theta = 0.05, \lambda = 1, \bar{g} = 0.05$	50.05
Pure transfer (PT) $\theta = 0.05, \lambda = 0, \bar{g} = 0.05$	6.42
Matched tied transfer (MTT) $\theta = 0.025, \lambda = 1, \bar{g} = 0.075$	44.90
Matched pure transfer (MPT) $\theta = 0.025, \lambda = 0, \bar{g} = 0.075$	26.82
TT > MTT > MPT > PT	
B. Unitary substitution in production: $\sigma = 1$	
Tied transfer (TT) $\theta = 0.05, \lambda = 1, \bar{g} = 0.05$	9.83
Pure transfer (PT) $\theta = 0.05, \lambda = 0, \bar{g} = 0.05$	8.32
Matched tied transfer (MTT) $\theta = 0.025, \lambda = 1, \bar{g} = 0.075$	5.07
Matched pure transfer (MPT) $\theta = 0.025, \lambda = 0, \bar{g} = 0.075$	5.35
TT > PT > MPT > MTT	
C. Perfect substitution in production: $\sigma \cong \infty$	
Tied transfer (TT) $\theta = 0.05, \lambda = 1, \bar{g} = 0.05$	−2.42
Pure transfer (PT) $\theta = 0.05, \lambda = 0, \bar{g} = 0.05$	9.82
Matched tied transfer (MTT) $\theta = 0.025, \lambda = 1, \bar{g} = 0.075$	−7.34
Matched pure transfer (MPT) $\theta = 0.025, \lambda = 0, \bar{g} = 0.075$	−1.27
PT > MPT > TT > MTT	

aid program when (i) the cost of borrowing increases (measured by an increase in a across a row) and (ii) the elasticity of substitution increases (measured by an increase in σ down a column). Therefore, $a = 0.02$ implies a low cost of borrowing from international capital markets, and $a = 10$ implies that the agent has virtually little or no access to international capital markets. The range of σ we consider is from 0.33 to 4. We consider three values for investment costs for public capital, with $h_2 = 1$, 15, and 50 signifying low, medium, and very high costs of installing public capital. For example, in Table 4A, when $h_2 = 1$, $a = 0.02$, and $\sigma = 0.8$, the welfare gain from an untied transfer is 8.27%, whereas from a tied transfer it is 34.52%. The following observations can be drawn from Tables 4A–4C.

(i) An increase in the elasticity of substitution always increases the welfare gains resulting from a PT. It reduces the welfare gains resulting from a TT, and indeed it may lead to a welfare loss if the installation costs associated with public capital are sufficiently large. The effects of TTs are much more sensitive to

Table 4. *Welfare sensitivity to installation costs, capital market imperfections, and degree of substitutability ($\theta = 0$ to $\theta = 0.05$; $\lambda = 1$)*

	$\alpha = 0.02$		$\alpha = 0.10$		$\alpha = 10$	
	$\lambda = 0$	$\lambda = 1$	$\lambda = 0$	$\lambda = 1$	$\lambda = 0$	$\lambda = 1$
A. Low installation costs ($h_2 = 1$)						
$\sigma = 0.33$	5.31%	90.39%	6.33%	56.55%	6.64%	48.47%
$\sigma = 0.8$	8.27%	34.52%	7.70%	21.28%	7.57%	19.84%
$\sigma = 1$	9.79%	26.54%	**8.06%**	**16.27%**	7.73%	15.32%
$\sigma = 1.2$	11.16%	22.12%	8.32%	13.38%	7.82%	12.64%
$\sigma = 4$	19.33%	12.19%	9.13%	6.21%	8.08%	5.75%
B. Medium installation costs ($h_2 = 15$)						
$\sigma = 0.33$	5.38%	84.76%	6.42%	50.05%	6.75%	42.06%
$\sigma = 0.8$	8.52%	26.90%	7.91%	14.81%	7.77%	13.86%
$\sigma = 1$	10.17%	17.99%	**8.32%**	**9.83%**	7.96%	9.47%
$\sigma = 1.2$	11.66%	12.72%	8.59%	6.96%	8.07%	6.87%
$\sigma = 4$	21.09%	−2.67%	9.50%	−0.36%	8.37%	0.07%
C. High installation costs ($h_2 = 50$)						
$\sigma = 0.33$	5.56%	69.87%	6.68%	32.95%	7.03%	25.33%
$\sigma = 0.8$	9.22%	5.51%	8.51%	−2.61%	8.35%	−1.99%
$\sigma = 1$	11.24%	−6.55%	**9.02%**	**−7.56%**	8.60%	−6.08%
$\sigma = 1.2$	13.16%	−14.82%	9.38%	−10.46%	8.76%	−8.53%
$\sigma = 4$	27.30%	−52.59%	10.59%	−16.65%	9.20%	−15.15%

σ than are those of PTs, and the sensitivity of both decreases with α.

The intuition underlying this key result is as follows. A PT has no effect on the stocks of public or private capital; all that happens is that consumption increases, raising the C/Y ratio. The higher elasticity of substitution raises the level of output attainable from given stocks of capital, thereby raising consumption and welfare uniformly. If the transfer is tied, the transfer increases the rate of investment in public capital. With a low elasticity of substitution, this requires an approximately corresponding increase in private capital, leading to a large increase in output, consumption, and benefits. As the elasticity of substitution increases, the higher public capital is associated with a larger decline of private capital so that the increase in output, consumption, and welfare declines. With very high installation costs, the TT is committing the recipient economy to devote a large portion of its resources to the costly task of installation, thereby making it worse off.

Other observations can be seen from Table 4:

(ii) Unless σ is very low, the benefits from pure aid decrease with the cost of borrowing. As long as tied aid yields positive benefits, these decrease with the cost of borrowing. In the cases where σ and h_2 are both high, so that tied aid leads to welfare losses, these losses decline with the cost of borrowing.

(iii) Irrespective of the cost of borrowing, and elasticity of substitution, the benefits from tied aid decrease and those from untied aid increase with installation costs.

(iv) Even though the magnitude of welfare gains from tied aid are generally higher than those from untied aid, for high values of σ ($= 4$), an untied aid program is strictly better than a tied aid program. This observation, along with observation (i), suggest that countries with a low elasticity of substitution between public and private capital in production may be better off with tied aid, whereas countries having a high degree of substitutability may benefit more from aid programs that are untied.

(v) When installation costs are high ($h_2 = 50$), an untied transfer is better than a tied transfer even for $\sigma = 1$ (the Cobb–Douglas case), when the latter is unambiguously welfare-deteriorating.

(vi) If we consider $\sigma = 1$ and $\alpha = 0.10$ as benchmark values, then even small deviations of σ from the benchmark (in the range 0.8–1.2) lead to substantial variations in welfare changes from both types of aid programs, irrespective of the cost of adjustment.

6. CONCLUSIONS

This chapter has characterized the effectiveness of a tied and untied aid program and the dynamic response it evokes in the recipient economy. We find that the long-run impact of a tied aid program and the direction of transitional dynamics it generates depend crucially on the elasticity of substitution in production. Our numerical simulations suggest that tied aid is more effective in economies with a low degree of substitution between factors of production. Moreover, the welfare gains from a tied or untied aid shock are sensitive to the substitutability of inputs, capital market imperfections, and costs of adjustment. These findings imply that when donors decide on whether a particular aid program should be tied to an investment activity, careful attention must be paid to the recipient's opportunities for substitution in production, its access to world capital markets, and the costs of installing the particular type of capital to which the aid will be tied.

REFERENCES

Arrow, K. J., and M. Kurz (1970), *Public Investment, the Rate of Return, and Optimal Fiscal Policy*, Johns Hopkins University Press, Baltimore.

Arrow, K. J., H. B. Chenery, B. S. Minhas, and R. M. Solow (1961), "Capital-Labor Substitution and Economic Efficiency," *Review of Economics and Statistics* 43: 225–50.

Aschauer, D. A. (1989a), "Is Public Expenditure Productive?" *Journal of Monetary Economics* 23: 177–200.

Aschauer, D. A. (1989b), "Does Public Capital Crowd Out Private Capital?" *Journal of Monetary Economics* 24: 171–88.

Auerbach, A. J., and L. J. Kotlikoff (1987), *Dynamic Fiscal Policy*, Cambridge University Press, Cambridge, UK.

Bardhan, P. K. (1967), "Optimal Foreign Borrowing," in K. Shell (ed.), *Essays on the Theory of Optimal Economic Growth*, MIT Press, Cambridge, MA.

Barro, R. J. (1990), "Government Spending in a Simple Model of Endogenous Growth," *Journal of Political Economy* 98: 103–25.

Barro, R. J., and X. Sala-i-Martín (1995), *Economic Growth*, McGraw-Hill, New York.

Baxter, M., and R. G. King (1993), "Fiscal Policy in General Equilibrium," *American Economic Review* 83: 315–34.

Berndt, E. R. (1976), "Reconciling Alternative Estimates of the Elasticity of Substitution," *Review of Economics and Statistics* 58: 59–68.

Bhagwati, J. N. (1967), "The Tying of Aid," in J. N. Bhagwati and R. S. Eckaus (eds.), *Foreign Aid*, Penguin, Harmondsworth, pp. 235–93.

Bhagwati, J. N., R. A. Brecher, and T. Hatta (1983), "The Generalized Theory of Transfers and Welfare: Bilateral Transfers in a Multilateral World," *American Economic Review*, vol. 73, 606–18.

Bhandari, J. S., N. U. Haque, and S. J. Turnovsky (1990), "Growth, External Debt, and Sovereign Risk in a Small Open Economy," *IMF Staff Papers* 37: 388–417.

Bond, E. W., P. Wang, and C. K. Yip (1996), "A General Two-Sector Model of Endogenous Growth with Human and Physical Capital: Balanced Growth and Transitional Dynamics," *Journal of Economic Theory* 68: 149–73.

Brakman, S., and C. van Marrewijk (1998), *The Economics of International Transfers*, Cambridge University Press, Cambridge.

Burnside, C., and D. Dollar (2000), "Aid, Policies, and Growth," *American Economic Review* 90: 847–68.

Cassen, R. (1986), *Does Aid Work?* Clarendon Press, Oxford.

Chatterjee, S., G. Sakoulis, and S. J. Turnovsky (2003), "Unilateral Capital Transfers, Public Investment, and Economic Growth," *European Economic Review*, 47, 1077–1103.

Devarajan, S., D. Xie, and H. Zou (1998), "Should Public Capital Be Subsidized or Provided?" *Journal of Monetary Economics* 41: 319–31.

Djajic, S., S. Lahiri, and P. Raimondos-Moller (1999), "Foreign Aid, Domestic Investment and Welfare," *The Economic Journal*, 109(October): 698–707.

Duffy, J., and C. Papageorgiou (2000), "A Cross-Country Empirical Investigation of the Aggregate Production Function Specification," *Journal of Economic Growth* 5: 87–120.

Eaton, J., and M. Gersovitz (1989), "Country Risk and the Organization of International Capital Transfer," in G. Calvo, R. Findlay, P. Kouri, and J. Braga de Macedo (eds.), *Debt, Stabilization and Development: Essays in Memory of Carlos Diaz-Alejandro*, Blackwell, Oxford, UK.

Edwards, S. (1984), "LDC Foreign Borrowing and Default Risk: An Empirical Investigation 1976–80," *American Economic Review* 74: 726–34.

European Union (1998a), *Council Regulation for an Instrument for Structural Policies for Pre-Accession*. Draft Proposal.

European Union (1998b), *Commission Communication to the Council and to the European Parliament on the Establishment of a New Financial Perspective for the Period 2000–2006*.

Fisher, W. H., and S. J. Turnovsky (1998), "Public Investment, Congestion, and Private Capital Accumulation," *Economic Journal* 108: 339–413.

Futagami, K., Y. Morita, and A. Shibata (1993), "Dynamic Analysis of an Endogenous Growth Model with Public Capital," *Scandinavian Journal of Economics* 95(4): 607–25.

Galor, O., and H. M. Polemarchakis (1987), "Intertemporal Equilibrium and the Transfer Paradox," *Review of Economic Studies* 54: 147–56.

Gang, I. N., and H. A. Khan (1990), "Foreign Aid, Taxes, and Public Investment," *Journal of Development Economics* 34: 355–69.

Glomm, G., and B. Ravikumar (1994), "Public Investment in Infrastructure in a Simple Growth Model," *Journal of Economic Dynamics and Control* 18: 1173–87.

Gramlich, E. M. (1994), "Infrastructure Investment: A Review Essay," *Journal of Economic Literature* 32: 1176–96.

Hatzipanayotou, P., and M. S. Michael (2000), "The Financing of Foreign Aid and Welfare: Income versus Consumption Tax," *Review of Development Economics* 4: 21–38.

Hayashi, F. (1982), "Tobin's Marginal and Average q: A Neoclassical Interpretation," *Econometrica* 50: 213–24.

Hulten, C. R. (1996), "Infrastructure Capital and Economic Growth: How Well You Use It May Be More Important Than How Much You Have," NBER Working Paper 5847.

Keynes, J. M. (1929), "The German Transfer Problem," *Economic Journal* 39: 1–7.

Khan, H. A., and E. Hoshino (1992), "Impact of Foreign Aid on the Fiscal Behavior of LDC Governments," *World Development* 20: 1481–88.

Lucas, R. E. (1988), "On the Mechanics of Economic Development," *Journal of Monetary Economics* 22: 3–42.

Lynde, C., and J. Richmond (1993), "Public Capital and Long-Run Costs in U.K. Manufacturing," *Economic Journal* 103: 880–93.

Obstfeld, M. (1982), "Aggregate Spending and the Terms of Trade: Is There a Laursen–Metzler Effect?" *Quarterly Journal of Economics* 97: 251–70.

Ohlin, B. G. (1929), "Transfer Difficulties, Real and Imagined," *Economic Journal* 39: 172–78.

Ortigueira, S., and M. S. Santos (1997), "On the Speed of Convergence in Endogenous Growth Models, *American Economic Review* 87: 383–99.

Pitchford, J. D. (1960), "Growth and the Elasticity of Substitution," *Economic Record* 36: 491–504.

Rebelo, S. (1991), "Long-Run Policy Analysis and Long-Run Growth," *Journal of Political Economy* 94: 1002–37.

Roubini, N., and P. Wachtel (1998), "Current Account Sustainability in Transition Economies," NBER Working Paper 6468.

Sachs, J. (1984), "Theoretical Issues in International Borrowing," *Princeton Studies in International Finance* 54.

Turnovsky, S. J. (1997a), "Public and Private Capital in an Endogenously Growing Open Economy," in B. S. Jensen and K. Y. Wong (eds.), *Dynamics, Economic Growth, and International Trade*, University of Michigan Press, Ann Arbor, MI.

Turnovsky, S. J. (1997b), "Public and Private Capital in an Endogenously Growing Economy," *Macroeconomic Dynamics* 1: 615–39.

Turnovsky, S. J. (2000), *Methods of Macroeconomic Dynamics*, Second Edition. MIT Press, Cambridge, MA.

Turunen-Red, A. H., and A. D. Woodland (1988), "On the Multilateral Transfer Problem: Existence of Pareto Improving International Transfers," *Journal of International Economics* 25: 249–69.

World Bank (1994), *World Development Report 1994: Infrastructure for Development*, Oxford University Press, New York.

8

Microchurning with Smooth Macro Growth:
Two Examples

Ronald W. Jones

Macroeconomic models of economies in the growth process are most often highly aggregated. There is no doubt that many variations at the detailed microeconomic level can yield the same overall macrolevels of growth, perhaps remaining fairly constant at high levels for years if not decades. However, the smooth aggregate levels may disguise rather interesting churning activity at the microlevel, with compositional changes that are not accidental and may, indeed, help to maintain high overall levels of growth. Here I wish mainly to consider two examples of this phenomenon, one focused on international trade and the other on technology.[1]

1. INTERNATIONAL TRADE AND CHURNING AT THE MICROLEVEL

By definition, a country that engages in international trade forsakes the kind of balanced growth associated with autarky, with local production responding to local demand. However, in simple textbook models of international trade that limit production and consumption to two commodities, it is possible to consider a balanced expansion in the composition of a country's production levels, with aggregate growth rates matched by those in each sector. What is missing in this account is the potential of international trade to allow (or force) a country to produce only a narrow range of products for the world market while consuming a wide variety of commodities, some requiring higher capital–labor ratios than found in home production and others that would utilize more

---

[1] John Pitchford invited me to Canberra to give a summer course in 1967, and on this occasion we had many talks about topics of mutual interest, including international trade and the role of technology.

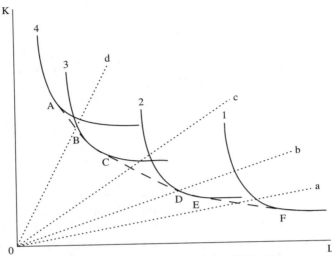

Figure 1. The Hicksian Composite Unit-Value Isoquant.

labor-intensive techniques than endowment ratios available at home. Furthermore, economic growth usually entails rising levels of *per capita* income, often accompanied by net investment (either from local savings or from foreign sources) and perhaps by improvements in technology. Here I concentrate on the former possibility, namely that an open economy with endowments of two factors, labor and capital, succeeds over time in accumulating capital while keeping population relatively in check. Leaving aside changes in the terms of trade stemming from alterations in production or demand in world markets, consider the sectoral changes at the microlevel that might accompany overall growth at a fairly constant level.

Trade theorists often use the *Hicksian composite unit-value isoquant* diagram to describe this setting. Figure 1 illustrates how growth in a country's overall capital–labor ratio can severely alter the composition of its production for world markets. Explicitly shown are unit-value isoquants for four different world-traded commodities. The *convex hull* of this set, the locus ABCDEF (extended at each end), consists of sections of individual unit-value isoquants (e.g., BC or DE), as well as linear segments involving production of two commodities (e.g., AB or CD). The nickname often used to describe this locus is "the best way of earning a buck in world markets." Four alternative rays from the origin are drawn, with each ray illustrating a particular overall capital–labor ratio available in this economy. For example, at the low ratio illustrated by ray *a*, this country's production patterns consists of fairly equal shares of commodities 1 and 2. Consider a smooth growth of the capital–labor endowment ratio from ray 0*a* to ray 0*b*. At first, growth of output in sector 2 is associated with a release of factors from the first sector with no change in the intensities used in each. That is, the increase in the capital–labor endowment ratio is totally absorbed by the change in the composition of outputs, with commodity 2 increasing and commodity 1 falling. At point E the first sector has completely shut down. As capital accumulation continues, until point D (along ray 0*b*) is reached, the economy is completely specialized in producing the second commodity and its rate of growth matches that of the economy as an aggregate. (I am ignoring the existence of non-traded commodities.) Growth in the second sector is positive all the way from ray 0*a* to ray 0*b*, although in the initial phase the growth rate in the second sector is higher than in the DE stretch because it is not only absorbing all the new capital supplied, but taking resources of both capital and labor away from the first sector as well. As further accumulation proceeds from ray 0*b* to 0*c*, output in the second sector goes into decline while the third sector witnesses rates of growth much larger than that of the economy's national income. Finally, from ray 0*c* to 0*d*, the third commodity initially experiences more rapid rates of growth than it registers in the BC range, in which it is the only commodity produced, and then suffers declines until, along ray 0*d*, it produces about the same fraction of the national income as it did earlier along ray 0*c*.

The growth pattern in this simple setting in which capital and labor are the only two factor inputs must be such that if only one commodity is produced its growth rate matches that of the aggregate, but if more than one commodity is produced (and more than two is not required, unless commercial policies or transport costs provide an umbrella of protection), it must be the case that the overall growth rate is flanked by higher rates for an expanding sector and *negative* rates of growth for the other participant sector.[2] Note how this churning activity as a consequence of the country being engaged in international trade would not be found in a closed economy in which growth of incomes would

---

[2] This is an expression of the Rybczynski effect (1955) for the growth of capital with a stable labor force at given commodity prices (along the flat segments in Figure 1).

spill over to encourage growth in all sectors, perhaps not at the same rate.[3] With a growing country embedded in a world trading community, capital accumulation could lead to steady overall rates of growth, but churning activity at the microlevel is a natural consequence of the country losing its comparative advantage in some sectors while gaining it in others. The successful growth experience of the Asian tigers in the past few decades illustrates (e.g., in Taiwan) how one-time leading sectors such as labor-intensive footwear or umbrellas shrink in the face of competition from other countries (e.g., China) as new industries (such as electronics and computer-related products) loom larger in national output. The point is not that such churning activity among sectors of production is possible; instead it is a natural consequence of countries being actively engaged in world trade. The composition of production with trade is no longer tied to the fairly stable composition of national demands.

2. FOLLOWERS LEAPFROGGING LEADERS

Turning now to technology, consider the situation in a particular industry within a country. Typically there will be leading firms and following firms – suppose the leaders have established their position by having been in the industry for a longer period of time and thus having proceeded farther along a learning curve. There is a particular class of technology currently relevant to producers in the industry, and I label this the θ-technology.[4] However, this industry is only one of many, and in each efforts are being expended in research and development with new ideas emerging. Some of these ideas have spillover value to other industries because advances in technology need not be limited in their relevance to the industry or firms in which they are developed. I am assuming that in the particular industry in which leading and follower firms are found many of these ideas from the rest of the economy have little relevance, but there may be some externalities that are of value. In particular, I consider an alternative class of technologies, the β-technology, that initially has no advantage over the currently used θ-technology, but if adopted in place of the θ-technology would, with

---

[3]   There may also be relative price changes that occur with growth of capital as well as the possibility of inferior goods in consumption.

[4]   This account, and Figure 2, rely heavily on Michihiro Ohyama and Ronald W. Jones (1995).

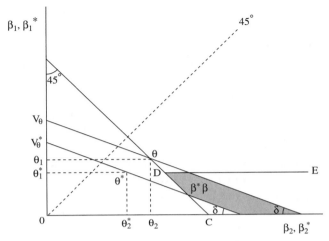

Figure 2. Leapfrogging Possibilities.

sufficient learning, prove to be superior in a future period. As a consequence both firms might switch to the β-technology, or both firms might conclude that the costs are too high and stay with the θ-technology, or one firm might switch and not the other. It is this latter possibility that is of interest, especially because an asymmetry in firm choice can often lead to the follower overtaking the other firm and emerging as the industry leader, even when both firms do not suffer any myopia that prevents them from seeing the future outcome of their choices.

Figure 2 illustrates the possibilities in a two-period setting. Let the vertical axis measure the productivities of the two alternative technologies in period 1, whereas the horizontal axis represents the values of the β- and θ-technologies in the second (and final) period. The figures of interest all lie below the constructed 45° ray, reflecting the power of the learning curve–productivities in general in period 2 are higher than in the first period. I choose an asterisk to distinguish the follower firm from the initially leading firm so that with the current θ-technology the leader's θ dominates that of the follower's θ^* for both periods. That is, the leader would maintain that position throughout with this technology. A pair of downward-sloping straight lines through the θ and θ^* points has been drawn. These lines allow the vertical intercepts, V_θ and V_θ^*, to denote the present discounted values of the two θ-productivities since the slopes of the lines depict the discount factors,

δ and δ^*, here taken to be the same for the two countries. For example, $V_\theta = \theta_1 + \delta\theta_2$.

The points representing the β-technology for the two countries could in principle be anywhere in the diagram. To illustrate the possibility of asymmetry in firm selection, they have been selected such that (i) both β_1 and β_1^* are inferior even to the follower's net productivity in the current period, θ_1^*; (ii) in the next period both β_2 and β_2^* exceed what the net productivity of the leader would be in that period if it had stayed with the θ-technology; (iii) the *undiscounted* sum of the β-technologies over both periods would exceed the undiscounted sum of the θ-technology over the two periods for the leader; and (iv) finally, I assume that the leader not only has superior knowledge of the θ-technology, but also would have an *absolute advantage* over the follower in the new β-technology in both periods. Thus the β points lie above a negatively sloped 45° line through the leader's θ point, and β lies northeast of β^*.

These restrictions cause the β and β^* points to lie in the triangular area, CDE, in Figure 2. Now consider the shaded region, in which the present discounted value of the follower's β^* point exceeds that for the original θ-technology, given by V_θ^*, but the present discounted value of the leader's β point falls short of that of its original θ-technology. As a consequence, the follower firm switches from the θ to the β technology, which proves to be less productive in the current period but makes up for this in the future with greater productivity. By contrast, the leader finds that the new β-technology is an inferior choice for it and so stays with the θ-technology. As a consequence, in period 2 the net productivity of the original follower, β_2^*, exceeds that of the leader, θ_2. The original follower becomes the leader.

This process of overtaking or leapfrogging is an example of the principle of *comparative advantage*. What is the cost of switching to the new technology for the follower? The current loss in productivity would be $(\theta_1^* - \beta_1^*)$, whereas the future gain would be $(\beta_2^* - \theta_2^*)$, so that the relative cost of switching would be their ratio, $(\theta_1^* - \beta_1^*)/(\beta_2^* - \theta_2^*)$. This is lower than the comparable relative cost of switching for the current leader, $(\theta_1 - \beta_1)/(\beta_2 - \theta_2)$. That is, the current follower has a comparative advantage in the new β-technology relative to the current leader. And this is the case despite the assumption that the original leader has an absolute advantage in the new β-technology. It is just that its absolute advantage is not as great as it is in the current θ-technology.

Having "learned by doing" in one technology, and thus becoming a leader in it, paves the way for having a comparative *dis*advantage in the new technology.[5]

3. CONCLUDING REMARKS

These are but two examples in which the possibility exists of seemingly smooth growth from period to period at the same aggregate growth rate, but where, at the microlevel, there is systematic churning activity. In the first of these, international trade rids the economy of the necessity of producing all of the variety of commodities it wishes to consume and, as a consequence, allows a great degree of concentration of resources to the traded-goods sectors that utilize productive factors in the same proportions as found in local supplies. As the stock of capital per capita increases with growth, the composition of the output bundle in the traded sector systematically changes, with the country gaining a comparative advantage in new, more capital-intensive sectors than previously produced at the same time as losing its comparative advantage in more labor-intensive commodities. Thus, at the disaggregated level, not only are all sectors not growing at the same rate, but some sectors are actually in decline. In the second example the doctrine of comparative advantage again comes into play, but this time it is of relevance to the composition of firms within a productive sector. If asymmetries in productive capabilities are rooted in large part in being at different points along a learning curve, and if in other sectors of the economy new technologies are being developed that may have some applicability to the sector under consideration, would some of these new technologies ever be adopted by one firm and not another? Yes, and it is the originally leading firm, the one that has better mastered the current technology, that tends precisely for that very reason to have a comparative *dis*advantage in the new technology. Being relatively good at one task tends to make the other firm relatively good at a new way of doing things. Thus the process of leapfrogging, or overtaking of the leader by the current follower, is a natural phenomenon not necessarily tied to any myopia on the part of the firm being overtaken.

---

[5]   Ohyama and Jones (1995) considered a case in which each firm can devote only a *fraction* of its resources to using (and learning) the new technology. It is shown that if each firm does this, the original follower will devote a larger fraction of its resource base to the new technology.

Many years ago Paul Samuelson, in his presidential address to the International Economic Association (1969), recalled his earlier years as a member of the Society of Fellows at Harvard. In particular, he related being asked by the mathematician, Stanislaw Ulam, to name a proposition in the social sciences that was true but not trivial. According to Samuelson, it was only somewhat later that he thought of a good answer – the doctrine of comparative advantage. In this note I have tried to suggest a pair of instances in which this doctrine also suggests that at the microeconomic level it is natural to expect that activities or firms that are favored in one period of time may lose out in future years as a country grows or as new technologies become available.

REFERENCES

Ohyama, Michihiro, and Ronald W. Jones (1995), "Technology Choice, Overtaking and Comparative Advantage," *Review of International Economics* 3 (2): 224–34.

Rybczynski, T. M. (1955), "Factor Endowments and Relative Commodity Prices," *Economica* 22: 336–41.

Samuelson, Paul A. (1969), "The Way of an Economist," in P. A. Samuelson (ed.), *International Economic Relations: Proceedings of the Third Congress of the International Economic Association*, MacMillan, London.

Index